$2   Wi...

gratitude

cony.

Young people and the Youth Service

International Library of Social Policy

General Editor   Kathleen Jones
Professor of Social Administration
University of York

Arbor Scientiæ
Arbor Vitæ

A catalogue of the books available in the **International Library of Social
Policy** and other series of Social Science books published by Routledge
& Kegan Paul will be found at the end of this volume

Young people and the Youth Service

Anthony J. Jeffs

Routledge & Kegan Paul

London, Boston and Henley

First published in 1979
by Routledge & Kegan Paul Ltd
39 Store Street, London WC1E 7DD
Broadway House, Newtown Road,
Henley-on-Thames, Oxon RG9 1EN and
9 Park Street, Boston, Mass. 02108, USA
Set in Press Roman by
Hope Services, Abingdon
and printed in Great Britain by
Redwood Burn Ltd
Trowbridge & Esher

ISBN 0 7100 03471

Contents

Preface

The Youth Service is a marginal service concerned according to its own evaluation with the social education of adolescents who themselves enjoy what Parkin describes as a 'temporary and transitional status'.[1] It operates on a limited budget derived primarily from three sources. First, on the central and local government funds which are principally dispensed through the education service, a source of finance that is crucial for the maintenance of the Youth Service in its present form, but which amounts annually to less than half of one per cent of the overall educational budget. Second, from privately contributed monies, bequests, flag-days and sponsored events. Third, from the charges levied upon the clients via subscriptions, membership fees, entrance charges and from the surplus or profit that accrues from the sale of goods and services to clients. In addition to the financial income there is also a substantial hidden subsidy, for the Youth Service depends upon the recruitment of tens of thousands of individuals who are prepared to donate their time and skills to youth work either free of charge or for a remuneration that bears little relation to the hours and effort contributed. In its reliance upon the unpaid and largely untrained voluntary worker the Youth Service is somewhat unique as a social and educational agency.[2] It may at one and the same time be viewed as either an anachronistic remnant of earlier forms of social and welfare provision based upon an individual altruistic gift relationship, or as a harbinger of a future in which, according to Crossman: 'community services – professionally trained, but manned largely by part-time volunteers – will within a decade be running a large part of our welfare state.'[3]

Despite the long-proven ability of the Youth Service to recruit voluntary staff, currently estimated at around 400,000[4] it has remained a rather anonymous agency, rarely attracting more than the passing interest of the media, legislators or public administrators. Even the Aves Report[5] which was concerned with the role of the voluntary worker within the personal social services failed to examine the Youth Service as an effective example of what might be achieved by the integration of the voluntary and the professional. This tendency to overlook the Youth Service is reflected in the failure of academics to treat it as a potentially fruitful area for research. Certainly none have as yet thought it worth while to chart its history, evaluate its impact, or to initiate a debate that might in some way contribute to the formulation of a coherent philosophy capable of underpinning the activities of the Youth Service.

What follows is obviously in no way intended to compensate for the previously mentioned omissions, it is, however, an attempt first to isolate and then examine those elements that have contributed to the development of the contemporary structure of the Youth Service. In particular Chapter 2 endeavours to account for the apparent rejuvenation of the Youth Service that coincided with the publication of the Albemarle Report in 1960 and to relate this to the appearance of what has been described as a distinctive youth culture.

Chapter 3 in discussing aspects of contemporary Youth Service provision adopts a different approach which due to restrictions of time and space is both selective and topic based. The choices that emerged reflect a desire to concentrate upon areas of potential growth and conflict. Consequently certain elements of the voluntary sector in particular have been dealt with somewhat cursorily while considerable attention has been devoted to school-based youth work and to the current expansion in provision being funded by statutory agencies that administratively operate outside the orbit of the education service. Other areas, such as the role and influence of the political youth movements, the leisure patterns of those young people not attached to the Youth Service, the organizational linkages existing between the voluntary and statutory sectors and the curriculum of the various Youth Service agencies might equally have demanded attention. However, in an area where there remains such a paucity of academic material and where as a consequence policy decisions seem to be all too often arrived at in a vacuum, then it is inevitable that glaring omissions remain.

Acknowledgments

Without the special help of a number of individuals and colleagues this book, I am certain, would never have seen the light of day. So although I had originally intended to avoid causing them any embarrassment by linking their names to this publication it now appears on reflection somewhat churlish to ignore their very real contributions. In particular I would like to record my debt to Professor Kathleen Jones for her continuous help and encouragement throughout; to Eric Butterworth for his support in the early stages; to Ron McGraw and Jackie Apperley who, despite their own heavy workloads, always found time to discuss mine; finally to Sydney Holdsworth who, although he has never seen the manuscript and probably will disagree with much it says, did more than anyone to set me thinking about the youth service and its role.

1   The early years

The passing of the 1870 Education Act led to a significant shift in the style and emphasis of youth work. Henceforth the 'rescue'[1] and basic educational work such as the teaching of literacy and numeracy that had been an integral part of much of the earlier provision[2] began to be pushed into the background as clubs[3] and organizations began to turn to meeting the leisure needs of young people, and in doing so trying to overcome what they discerned as the deficiencies of the elementary school system.

Leisure itself came to be viewed by youth workers as a problem in its own right. As Dr J. Scott Lidgett, the founder of the Wesley Guild, put it, 'the sooner we recognise that recreation unorganised is a danger, the better.'[4] However, many of the youth organizations that emerged in the years following 1870 saw their work as far more all-embracing than that of merely filling the leisure time of the young. They were anxious above all else to offer their clients a set of religious and social values. They believed their role to be a crucial one, for they saw their clients as passing through:[5]

> the most important space in a human lifetime . . . the years during which the rest of the life is practically lost or won, a springtime of character at which the mind's most receptive and plastic, in which habits good or evil are being formed for life.

Values

The precise nature of the social values that the clubs and groups wished to impart to their members were often somewhat obscure. It was usually assumed that they were the birth-right of those born into the upper and middle classes, but were something that the young of the labouring and working classes might only acquire as a result of instruction. As the Hon. T.W.H. Pelham, the founder of the London Federation of Working Boys' Clubs explains, the purpose of these clubs was to offer the poor in some measure 'what the public schools and universities have been to the rich. They develop, as no other agency can, the esprit de corps, in

1

which the poor, for the most part, are so lamentably deficient'.[6] The assumption that the poor lacked certain desirable personal qualities and attributes is implicit in the remarks of Pelham. Sadly this was not atypical, and these sentiments were shared by many of his contemporaries in youth work.[7] In consequence they at times displayed some of the worst kind of class arrogance, and appeared to have overlooked many of the self-initiated efforts of working men and women to improve their conditions through mutual co-operation.[8] It is significant that the remarks of Pelham were first published in the same year as the Bryant and May match girls strike took place and only twelve months prior to the Great Dock Strike centred on the East End of London, the very area where Pelham worked. Compare Pelham's views with those of John Burns writing of his experiences during the dockers' strike:[9]

> labour of the humbler kind has shown its capacity to organise itself; its solidarity; its ability; its readiness to endure much for little gain ... I have never ceased to wonder all through the strike at the moderation and the honesty of the strikers. I have been in the thick of starving men, with hundreds of pounds about me (they knowing it), and not a penny have I lost. I have sent men whom I did not know, for change of a gold piece, and have never been cheated a penny. Not a man through all the weeks of that desperate strike ever asked me for drink money.

It is difficult to believe that Pelham and Burns are writing of experiences gathered in the same community, and the quotation from Burns appears to make nonsense of Pelham's assertion that the poor lack 'esprit de corps'. However, it would be unfair to dismiss out of hand the efforts of upper-class reformers and philanthropists such as Pelham, Hogg, Devine and Newman; although their views may often have been tinged with patronage and 'flavoured with a kind of piety' which now seems dated, that they did as Macalister Brew points out, make 'an incalculable contribution to the lives of many young people in an age when few cared for them is indisputable, and should not be lightly dismissed'.[10]

The growth of collectivism

In the last quarter of the nineteenth century a series of trade slumps and a relative decline in Britain's economic position[11] culminated in the economic crisis of the 1890s which 'gave Victorian courage and optimism the severest shock that it had yet received'.[12] The tensions brought to the surface by the faltering of the economy combined with the challenge to the system of a growing body of empirical evidence that clearly demonstrated the extent to which laissez-faire doctrines were incapable of providing solutions to the persistent and worsening social problems, helped to create a climate receptive to change,[13] and 'a general questioning and uncertainty about the course of social developments'.[14] One noticeable response to this development was an increased willingness on the part of enlightened public administrators and members of the professions, 'whose ideal society was a functional one based on expertise and selection by merit',[15] to examine the collectivist solutions to social problems offered by writers such as J.S. Mill, Bradley, T.H. Green and Bosanquet and of the Fabians who 'demanded a clean break with laissez-faire individualism'.[16]

The early Edwardian years saw no diminution in the process of change, and although they did witness an economic recovery this had to be balanced with the growing threat posed by Teutonic competition, both commercial and military, and the rising expectations of the organized labour movement which gave additional strength to those who advocated collectivist solutions to social problems. In particular, as Fraser points out, the small but influential groups of socialists, ranging from the revolutionaries of the SDF (Social Democratic Federation) to the gradualists of the Fabian Society, had a profound effect upon both Conservatives and Liberals alike. The socialists 'became a sort of bogeyman to haunt the politicians and stimulate their social concern'.[17] Balfour, the Conservative leader, reflected this concern in a speech he made in 1895, during which he outlined his attitude towards social legislation:[18]

> it (social legislation) is not merely to be distinguished from Socialist legislation but it is its most direct opposite and its most effective antidote. Socialism will never get possession of the great body of public opinion . . . among the working class or any other class if those who wield the collective forces of the community show themselves desirous to ameliorate every legitimate grievance and to put society upon a proper and more solid basis.

In the educational sphere the attitudes that underpinned the views expressed by Balfour generated major and wide-ranging reforms, payment by result gradually disappeared, new subjects entered the curriculum of elementary schools, technical education was encouraged and the administration of both secondary and higher education was totally transformed by the 1902 Education Act. In terms of social legislation it led the Conservatives to enact the Workman's Compensation Act of

1897, which Titmuss has singled out as 'the first instalment of what we now call "Social Security".'[19] When this view was harnessed to the widespread concern aroused at the end of the Boer War by the publication of a report from the Inspector-General of Recruiting which spoke of the 'gradual deterioration of the physique of the working classes'[20] the pressure for social reform became almost unstoppable. The response of the new Liberal government elected in 1905 reflected this mood and they introduced a comprehensive body of legislation that created 'the outline of a system of social security'.[21]

The new welfare legislation inevitably eroded much of the power and influence of the COS (Charity Organisation Society) and the numerous Victorian charities and self-help groups, large and small, who had for so long been a central feature of welfare provision. In parts these groups can be seen as victims of their own success, for[22]

> the very professionalism of the C.O.S., through its intervention of caseworkers to examine the causes and remedies of poverty, uncovered depths of undeserved misery and want which could not be put down to the sins of the individual, and could not be cured by private charity, however well organised.

In many ways this analysis applied equally to the numerous youth work agencies who, often operating in the areas of most acute urban deprivation, had done so much to highlight the long-term effects of poverty upon the adolescent. The growing body of new welfare legislation and the changed social climate that both proceeded and accompanied it, may only have intruded upon the activities of the various organizations catering for the social and leisure needs of young people indirectly, but like the 1870 Education Act before they led to an inevitable shift in both the pattern and style of provision. Just as after 1870 youth work had become increasingly marginal in educational terms, so the new welfare legislation removed from youth work many of its few remaining 'rescue' functions.

This sense of marginality may have provoked, or been the result of, the adoption of self-imposed aims for youth work by many clubs and organizations that encouraged them to concern themselves overwhelmingly with the inculcation of intangible social and spiritual values amongst their clients rather than in improving their material well-being. Unable or unwilling to offer, or to meet, those material needs of the adolescent, youth work tended to distance itself from those movements and groups which were engaged in the struggle for more root and branch social reforms. Even committed social reformers, such as Octavia Hill,

who recognized the need for a youth work intervention, nevertheless
saw it almost exclusively as an agency through which the young might
be introduced to these values and in consequence came to view the
members largely as passive recipients. Octavia Hill summed up these
values when she sponsored an Army Cadet Force unit in the East End
of London in order that the young men who joined might benefit
from the 'exercise, discipline, obedience, esprit de corps, camping-out,
and manly companionship with the gentlemen who would be their
officers'.[23]

The uniformed youth organizations

The Army Cadet Force was the first of the many uniformed youth
organizations that were to establish themselves between 1860 and the
onset of the First World War,[24] and which were to radically alter both
the content and direction of youth work, their very success helping to
create a momentum that resulted in the bulk of youth work practice
becoming ideologically distanced from both mainstream social work
and education, despite the common roots shared by all three.

All the uniformed groups shared a close affinity with the Muscular
Christianity of Dr Thomas Arnold whose professed aim was to endow
boys with 'the bodies of men strong and active, their minds clear, rich
and versatile, and their spirits able to control both body and mind and
to direct their physical and mental powers to the service of God'.[25] This
formula may have been perfectly suited for boys living in the relatively
closed institutional setting of a public school but for young men who
spent their days in either elementary schools or paid employment
Arnold's construct was far too all embracing and comprehensive.
Youth workers therefore tended to leave the scholastic elements to
other agencies and to concentrate upon the 'character building' aspects,
nevertheless the debt to Arnold was substantial and readily acknowledged. William Smith, the founder of the Boys' Brigade, which was
easily the most influential of the early uniformed groups,[26] writing in
an early edition of its journal *The Boy* set out the priorities of that
organization, and in the process recognized the contribution of Arnold,
'character training strongly coloured by Arnoldian public school ideas,
was important more than the acquisition of textbook knowledge.'[27]

This belief coupled with a strong emphasis upon the inherent value
of drill and a public image of the Brigade conveyed by their uniform,
loosely adapted from that of the Lanarkshire Volunteers, a unit in which
Smith himself was a serving officer, led to the levelling of charges that

the Brigade was promulgating the twin evils of 'Prussianism and Militarianism'. Even within his own church Smith was vigorously attacked by fellow members who were opposed to what they saw as his attempt to train boys for militarism. A Non-Conformist group called the Peace Society exhorted its supporters to do their utmost to 'crush this young praying and fighting monster – the masterstroke of Mars . . . dragging true religion into the gutter of corruption'.[28] Like others before him and since Smith retorted that his purpose was simply to imbue in the elementary schoolboy that 'esprit de corps which public school boys acquire as a matter of course'.[29] However laudable his aims it is difficult to dismiss the charges laid against Smith as being without any foundation, for the stress placed upon the inherent value of drill and absolute discipline was such that the Brigade can hardly be said to have offered its members a balanced educational and leisure programme. Independence of spirit and mind were simply not encouraged, for in Smith's own words he envisaged that for a boy enlisting in the Brigade:[30]

> there is also developed a marked recognition of leadership and an un-
> swerving loyalty to his teachers . . . it is just this natural propensity
> which the Boys' Brigade seizes hold of. It first turns it to good
> account and then seeks to enlarge the scope of it . . . by forming the
> boys into companies under Christian men . . . to whom the boys can
> look as their trusted leaders. In the company they are banded
> together by drill and discipline which lays the best groundwork for a
> wholesome moral and religious training.

Smith gave the Boys' Brigade a programme based squarely upon what George VI was later to call 'The Twin Pillars of Religion and Discipline'.[31] It was to prove in terms of recruitment a highly successful formula and one that as previously noted was to be widely imitated. In part at least it was adopted by what was to become the most numerically successful of the pre-1914 youth organizations, the Boy Scouts.

The Boy Scouts were founded in 1907 by Robert Baden-Powell. The Scouts shared a great many common traits with the Boys' Brigade; Baden-Powell for example was encouraged to publish his manual 'Aids to Scouting'[32], the book that was to inspire the Scout movement, by Smith who had used it with Boys' Brigade companies. The two men were close personal friends up until the death of Smith in 1914, and Baden-Powell actually proposed a merger of the two organizations, but Smith rejected this overture no doubt because he correctly recognized that in many respects the differences between the two groups were as legion as the similarities.[33]

From the outset the Boy Scouts were, unlike the Boys' Brigade, independent of one particular religious denomination, maintaining a flexible attitude which, according to Baden-Powell, meant: 'We do not interfere with the boys' religion of whatsoever form it may be, though we encourage him to practice whichever he professes.'[34] The Scout troop might be attached to a church or chapel, but it could equally be linked to a school or be totally independent. Baden-Powell also had a different conception of discipline from that of Smith, viewing it very much as an inner quality best developed by encouraging efficiency and controlled independence. For this reason Baden-Powell regarded drill as educationally unsound and a poor medium for instruction, and in 'Scouting for Boys' he very clearly spells out what he sees as the 'evils' of drill:[35]

(1) Military drill gives a feeble, unimaginative officer a something with which to occupy his boys. He does not consider whether it appeals to them or really does them good. It saves him a world of trouble.

(2) Military drill tends to destroy individuality whereas we want in the Scouts to develop individual characters; and when once drill has been learned it bores a boy who is longing to be tearing about on some enterprise or other; it blunts his keenness. Of boys drilled in Cadet Corps under 10 per cent go into the Army afterwards. Our aim is to make young backwoodsmen of them, not imitation soldiers.

For these reasons I would not like to see any more of the dull routine of drill introduced into our training.

By laying considerable stress upon his own imperialistic background[36] Baden-Powell gave the Scouts a Kiplingesque air designed to capture some of the 'romance' of the Empire:[37]

Scoutcraft includes the qualities of our frontier colonists, such as resourcefulness, endurance, pluck, trustworthiness, etc., plus the chivalry of the knight . . . we supply a character education which does not come within the scope of the present book-instruction of the schools.

This dissatisfaction with the quality of the education offered by the elementary schools reflected the opinion expressed earlier by Smith, and might almost be taken as a back-handed compliment to the developing school system. For, as Elvin notes, by the Edwardian period the elementary schools had become very different institutions from their predecessors:[38]

there was no longer crude talk of keeping people in their proper stations and of educating them simply for the lot to which God had called them. The teachers themselves had built up their union and within an accepted social framework were increasingly self-respecting and self-reliant.

The Scouts and the other youth organizations were by the outbreak of the First World War effectively excluded from the school system. This encouraged many to adopt a largely critical attitude towards certain aspects of the school system, whilst others saw the separation as a fact of life and in consequence set about the task of defining a unique non-scholastic role for youth work, one that all too often tended to fall back upon abstract values most notably that of 'esprit de corps, the talisman phrase of the age'.[39] Education, thus for many, came to be defined as something which took place in the school[40] and social education or character building became the prerogative of external, voluntary agencies. The division was of course a false one, but one that has remained a powerful factor in youth work practice and a part explanation for the low status of youth work.

The growth of the Boy Scouts and its sister organization the Girl Guides was nothing less than phenomenal. Within two years of Baden-Powell holding the first camp on Brownsea Island it had acquired over 100,000 members (the Boys' Brigade had 54,000 members in 1908) and was operating in virtually every corner of the Empire as well as in such diverse countries as Chile, Denmark, Finland, France, Greece, Russia, Holland and the USA. This expansion continued unabated throughout the rest of the decade and by 1921 the Scouts had achieved a world-wide membership of over 1,000,000 spread throughout more than forty countries.[41]

The simple, not to say simplistic code and set of values promulgated by Baden-Powell seemed to have been acceptable wherever they travelled. Exhorting its members to[42]

> work for the good of your country, or for the business in which you are employed, and you will find that as you do this you will be getting all the promotion and all the success that you want . . . it is your duty to your country to improve yourself.

This code not surprisingly made the Scouts welcome to all but the most repressive national regimes,[43] for it is an 'a-political' message that in no way encourages its young members to challenge the status quo and the established orthodoxy by either word or deed.

Boys' clubs and girls' clubs

The success of the various uniformed groups and in particular that of
the Boy Scouts in the twenty years preceding the Great War, has tended
to overshadow the developments that took place during those years in
other areas of youth provision. In particular the continued expansion of
the Boys' Club Movement and the work of Charles Russell in forging a
national structure. Russell was especially anxious to provide facilities
for underprivileged urban adolescents and although his clubs and others
like them were not designed exclusively for the 'hordes of young black-
guards, who showed little promise of growing into anything better than
vagabonds and criminals'[44] the shortage of resources often led to an
emphasis being placed upon the needs of that group. Like the girls' clubs
that constituted the Girls' Club Union founded by Maude Stanley in
1883, Russell's clubs endeavoured to offer a leisure service for those
'deprived of the simplest privileges'.[45] An indication of the type of
youngster the boys' clubs established by Russell and his colleagues were
designed to cater for can be gained from Russell's practical hints as to
the outfitting of such clubs:[46]

> The windows should be frosted glass up to a man's height, or – and
> this is far more homely – should be fitted with blinds or curtains.
> For this purpose there is perhaps nothing better than crimson
> holland blinds with spring rollers . . . . Except to meet cases of
> emergency, such as fire, there should be only one means of entrance
> and exit. A club which members can enter or leave by two different
> doors is full of possibilities for all kinds of mischief . . . . The upper
> halves of all doors in the club should be glazed, the better to secure
> proper supervision . . . some boys, particularly untamed new
> members, are always on the qui vive to outwit their officers, and
> three or four lads often find great pleasure in 'sporting their oak',
> which means that gambling and other unauthorised proceedings may
> be taking place behind a closed door.

In spite of the efforts of Russell and his colleagues to increase the
number of clubs nationally and the expansion in the number of girls'
clubs in London, Dawes concludes that little, if any, overall expansion
took place between 1900 and 1914, due in part he suggests to a declining interest amongst Church of England clergy in London in club work.[47]
An indication of the extent to which, in London at least, the club
movement had by the 1900s lost its earlier impetus is conveyed by the
decline in the number of clubs affiliated to the London Federation of

Boys' Clubs, which fell from thirty-one in 1900 to ten in 1912. The problem was not exclusively related to the fall in the number of clubs, for many of those that survived showed a propensity to concentrate upon the achievement of high standards of sporting excellence,[48] a policy which meant that they found it advantageous to keep 'the rougher boys out'.[49] This left according to Dawes only four boys' clubs in London that were in 1914 catering for those drawn 'from the poorest homes'.

No evidence appears to indicate that the volume and quality of provision for girls exceeded that available for boys in 1914, or that the rapidly expanding uniformed groups were succeeding in doing more than recruit members from amongst those 'who were in the comity of the nation, who attended church or chapel, had decent and orderly homes and, as a rule, accepted the usages of society.'[50] Certainly Paul, writing of his early experiences in the Boy Scouts, gives an indication of the extent to which they aroused hostility rather than acceptance amongst the young people living in the poorer areas:[51]

> Every Sunday we formed up in military order in the cobbled stable-yard behind our waving flags and led by a shrilling drum and bugle band marched off to church. The Boy Scout movement was so new in those days that we were fair game. Crowds would follow the marching troop; not always friendly ones and often to march out of the stableyard we had to push through a mob of spitting and cheering youths from the nearby slum streets. They had a song about us which began:
>
> 'Here come the Brussel Sprouts,
> The stinking, blinking louts'

The First World War and after

The lack of youth provision particularly of the kind attractive to young people living in the poorer urban areas and the older adolescent became apparent during the First World War when, according to one social historian: 'a revolution in the age-sex earnings pattern took place, and marked the beginning of the trend leading to the affluent teenager of the 1960s'.[52] Young people of both sexes became beneficiaries of the war boom. The financial gains were however often secured at the cost of a lost education, for the Government to meet the increased demands of industry for labour cut short the schooling of over 600,000 young people by lowering the statutory leaving age.[53]

A combination of increased earning and spending power among adolescents, plus the weakening of family ties due to the war-time conditions, led in the words of one contemporary commentator to a 'grave increase in the numbers of juvenile offenders', to the extent that it was possible to talk of juvenile lawlessness spreading 'through the country like a plague'.[54] This 'crime-wave' coupled with a reported increase in levels of drunkenness and vandalism amongst both adolescents and juveniles was discussed at length in two reports published in 1917 by the National Council of Public Morals and the Board of Education Departmental Committee on Juvenile Delinquency[55] respectively.

The response of the Government to the growing 'youth problem' amounted to a series of measures that could be best described as a large stick and a small carrot. Magistrates were to be encouraged to impose more exemplary sentences on any juveniles who were brought before them and additional funds were earmarked to improve the policing of city areas to raise the detection rates. The end result of these two policy decisions may well have been counter-productive, for as a City of Westminster Probation Officer pointed out in 1917:[56]

> There has been a tendency in recent years to increase the variety of offences with which children may be charged. For instance children are now charged with wandering, with being without proper guardianship, with being 'beyond control'. Our streets are now more rigidly supervised than ever before. There is a large and increasing army of officials whose duty it is to watch over our child life. In many cases it has seemed to me that the zeal of those officers was not always tempered by humanity and expediency.

The somewhat diminutive carrot initially proffered by the Home Secretary was the setting up of a committee chaired by Charles Russell with the remit of examining the problem of juvenile crime and of recommending preventative measures that might be usefully undertaken by both the Government and the new Juvenile Organization it proposed to establish.

The Russell Committee[57] made a number of far-reaching and imaginative recommendations that were to prove the precursor of future direct governmental involvement in youth work. It advocated the setting up of local juvenile organization committees to co-ordinate and encourage the provision of facilities for young people, and that LEAs should be given the powers to enable them financially to support such committees and approved voluntary groups within their area. Regarding non-vocational adult education such powers already existed via the

1902 Education Act and the Board of Education Regulations for Technical Schools, both of which had proved flexible enough to allow the more imaginative LEAs to transfer small but often vital payments to such bodies as the WEA, however no such loopholes existed regarding youth provision. This anomaly was accepted as such by the Board and the Fisher Education Act of 1918 incorporated Russell's recommendation by investing in LEAs the powers to spend money on facilities for physical training and organized games, holiday camps and for the social training of young persons in the evening, which in essence meant that they could if they so desired make grants available to youth clubs and groups. The sections of the 1918 Act dealing with provision for the needs of working youth were subsequently augmented in the Board of Education Circular Number 86 issued in 1921, and this gave LEAs the powers to set up their own 'Juvenile Organizing Committees' where local voluntary organizations had not already done so.

In real terms despite their good intentions these initiatives achieved very little. The economic situation during the immediate post-war years was such that the funds were simply not available to allow LEAs to make any sizeable impact in the area of youth provision. The Great War 'had smashed the delicate framework of international economic and financial organisation which was the chief established instrument for guiding and easing adjustments to general economic changes',[58] and from this international crisis an internal one developed which obliged the Government to adopt harsh deflationary policies. Dubbed the 'Geddes Axe', after the chairman of the Government committee which reported in 1922 on ways in which public expenditure could be curtailed in order to alleviate the fiscal crisis, these cut-backs effectively ensured that the social policies advocated in the reports of the Ministry of Reconstruction achieved for that Ministry 'nothing except its own disappearance in the depression'.[59] In the educational sphere these economies resulted in the non-implementation of Fisher's proposal for the raising of the school-leaving age, in the postponing of the establishment of part-time day continuation schools,[60] in the non-implementation of the imaginative 1919 Report on adult education[61] and in a severe curtailment of LEA spending that virtually ensured that the proposed intervention of local government agencies in youth work were stillborn.

The Juvenile Organization Committees that were set up in the localities were starved of funds and 'withered through lack of support'[62] in all but a few areas where they 'survived to form the basis of the local youth committees'[63] that were to be established in 1941. It is not insignificant that the few which did prosper, most notably in Liverpool, Birmingham, Southampton, Edinburgh and Middlesbrough, were those which were 'used by the LEA as a channel for grants to juvenile organizations'.[64] Without the promise of financial aid it appears that the various voluntary agencies, large and small, could not be held together at a local level. Old habits of rivalry were often too deeply ingrained for them to evaporate as a result of mere exhortation; as Davies and Gibson point out, the various voluntary organizations 'opposed other possible types of provision and offered their own, because with deep sincerity they believed they were the best thing for the young.'[65]

Community centres and clubs between the wars

Despite the depressed state of the economy during much of the interwar period new areas of youth work were developed and old-established ones consolidated. For example, Henry Morris opened the first Cambridgeshire Village College designed to offer a comprehensive youth and community provision within one campus at Sawston in 1928; but it is indicative of the financial constraints of the period, that despite his drive and determination, and the apparent success of the venture, nearly a decade elapsed before sufficient funds could be raised for work to start on a second college.[66]

Another major innovation of long-term significance was the development of community centres. This largely followed from the founding of the 'New Estates Community Committee' (later entitled the 'Community Centres Association') in 1929 by the National Council for Social Service, the British Association of Residential Settlements and the Educational Settlements Association. This committee largely as a direct consequence of funding made available by the NCSS was able to distribute grants towards the cost of building and maintaining community centres on new council estates. The centres were designed to integrate youth and adult provision in one unit, and the success of this initiative led to the inclusion of Clause 80 in the 1936 Housing Act which conferred upon housing authorities the powers to enable them to make funds available for the construction and maintenance of community centres and recreation grounds for their tenants.

The new community centres were, as Cameron found, not always successful in providing for the needs of the communities they were designed to service. Some had youth centres attached, some endeavoured to integrate both youth and adult provision, whilst other centres compromised by building separate entrances and partitioning the building up between youth and adult users. However the end result almost invariably meant that young people 'tended to be crowded out by adult users'.[67] Morgan even went so far as to claim 'that practically no new community centre makes adequate provision for the needs of the adolescent. So far as inquiry has revealed the Slough Social Centre seems to be the only one.'[68]

The NCSS also made available grants of approaching £1,000,000[69] during the inter-war years for centres offering social and recreational facilities for the unemployed in those areas where this problem was most acute. These 'Occupational Centres' and 'Community Service Clubs' appear to have often been funded in order to provide an alternative to the facilities set up by the Communist led National Unemployed Workers' Movement[70] whose centres were viewed by the NCSS as 'potential threats to their own as well as to national stability'.[71] The NCSS funds were made available to existing centres upon the condition that the incumbent management committee was replaced by one 'composed of representatives of industry and commerce and public men of the district'[72] – in short, of men able and willing to exclude and isolate 'undesirable' political elements from the centre.

Hanson in his survey of the NCSS sponsored centres in Durham gives no indication as to their levels of success in attracting members. However Cameron *et al.* in their study of unemployed youth found that only 6 per cent of their sample attended such centres. Interestingly they found that the 'absence of democratic control provided the ground for the most serious of the criticisms offered by the young men on the conduct of the Centres.'[73] Certainly Cameron *et al.* found that the two centres in Pontypridd, where over 20 per cent of those interviewed were members, were not only far and away the most successful in terms of attendance, but significantly they were also unique in that they were the only centres 'in which the members had a fair measure of responsibility for control and management'.[74] Judging from the limited evidence of the Cameron *et al.* survey the centres were not a success, but the paternalistic management was not the only inhibiting factor, for the young people in the survey were also highly critical of the staid and unimaginative programme of activities they offered.[75]

The NCSS financed 'Occupational Centres' and 'Community Service Clubs' catered only for unemployed males aged eighteen and over, their equivalent for the under-eighteens were the 'Juvenile Instruction Centres'. These were first established by the Ministry of Labour in November 1918 and by early 1919 over 200 were in operation with over 24,000 young people in daily attendance. Unemployment amongst juveniles declined sharply after 1920 and the centres were phased out during that year.[76] By 1923 however juvenile unemployment was once more becoming a serious problem and six new centres were opened in that year followed by a further 109 in the following year. Attendance was voluntary until 1934 when the Unemployment Act passed in that year laid down that every boy and girl under eighteen who was neither at school or in full-time employment could be required to attend a JIC. From the outset the centres were beset with difficulties that were not solved even after 1934 and the introduction of compulsory attendance. First, many young people did not bother to register with authorities as unemployed which meant that many districts failed to qualify for Ministry of Labour grants even though they had high levels of juvenile unemployment. Second, the Ministry insisted that the daily attendance at a given centre must not fall below forty which meant that many centres were often closed and then re-opened only to close again shortly afterwards as unemployment rates fluctuated, while others had their status altered from that of a grant aided centre to that of a class which meant a reduction in contact hours from fifteen hours per week to six. Not surprisingly, given the regulations under which they were obliged to operate, local authorities who were delegated to run the centres and classes found it difficult to recruit suitably qualified staff even in areas of high unemployment, and were themselves often reluctant 'to embark on the administrative work necessary to establish classes or centres when they could be closed in circumstances over which the authority had no control whatsoever'.[77]

The response amongst young people to the centres and classes was on the whole 'disappointing'[78] and this was undoubtedly a factor in persuading the Government to make attendance compulsory. A number of LEAs sought alternatives to compulsion, Lancashire for example allowed those who enrolled for an ordinary evening class to be excused attendance, while Whitehaven in Cumbria maintained that it was socially wrong to establish institutions which segregated and branded unemployed adolescents and in consequence refused to set up any centres or classes in their area. The centres were according to Morgan the end product of a 'half-hearted policy'[79] and certainly they appear to have been only markedly successful 'in places like the pit villages of South Wales or County Durham where the permanency and virtual universality of unemployment socialised the community into accepting and participating in the facilities and activities provided'.[80] Nevertheless the centres and the classes, for all their failings, were an intervention by central government designed to offer a positive alternative to 'loafing in the streets'[81] and as such were an indication of the increasing willingness of government agencies to involve themselves in the provision of facilities for the adolescent.

The growth of government intervention

Whether in the form of direct funding, as in the case of the junior instruction centres or indirectly via the NCSS, the Government came to play during the inter-war period an increasingly significant part in the provision of youth facilities. Likewise local authorities, who following the false dawn of Circular 86 gradually became more and more prominent in the field, either through their involvement in the provision of community centres and recreational areas or as in a limited number of areas, through their support of voluntary youth work initiatives with grant-aid. However it is important not to over emphasize the role played by central and local government prior to 1939, for the bulk of youth work was still overwhelmingly carried out by voluntary organizations dependent upon their own ability to raise finance and recruit unpaid voluntary staff.

The voluntary workers estimated at between 125,000[82] and 140,000[83] outnumbered the 120 or so[84] full-time paid youth leaders by over 1,000 to 1. The dependence upon the volunteer resulted, according to Rooff, in 'many a club languishing for want of trained and experienced leaders',[85] and provision remaining 'a haphazard mixture of philanthropy, government and, self-help and voluntary enthusiasm'.[86] Certainly many of the voluntary organizations were weakest in the areas of greatest social need, for in those areas not only were local communities least able to finance new initiatives but also the class structure meant 'that the so-called leisured class from which the whole-time worker of the past'[87] had been recruited were rarely to be found. The Government recognized this problem and in 1934 the Special Areas Commissioner began making grants to voluntary organizations to enable them to develop their work in the depressed areas. The results as Dawes notes were often quite dramatic:[88]

> Without the Depression there might have been no boys' clubs in Durham. By 1937 there were forty-four affiliated to the county association, where three years before there had been only eight and, six years previously, none at all.

The major youth organizations that had dominated youth provision at the end of the First World War remained pre-eminent throughout the

inter-war period. In terms of membership the boys' and girls' clubs affiliated to the NABC (National Association of Boys' Clubs) and the NCGC
(National Council of Girls' Clubs) were the most substantial providers
followed by the various uniformed groups of which the Boy Scouts
and the Girl Guides were easily the largest. With regards to recruitment the Boys' Club Movement was probably the most successful
youth organization during the inter-war period doubling its membership
during the 1930s alone,[89] while the Scouts and Guides after a period of
slow but unspectacular growth appeared to have stabilized their membership at around 200,000 apiece after 1935. It is important to note
that none of the voluntary organizations catered exclusively for the
over-fourteens, all tending to recruit the bulk of their members from
below what is now the statutory age in local authority clubs. Obviously
the percentage of members over fourteen varied considerably not only
between organizations but probably from area to area, nationally however, by 1938, the NABC with 50 per cent of its members over fourteen
was the most successful of the major voluntary groups in this respect,
while the Girl Guides with 16 per cent appears to have been the least
successful.[90]

A number of voluntary groups during the inter-war years began
seriously to decline. The Church Lads' Brigade, the Catholic Lads'
Brigade and the Cadet Forces all suffered from sharply falling membership. The latter group in particular were the victims of a growing anti-
militarist feeling in certain quarters which led to a number of LEAs
closing OTC units attached to their schools, with the result that 'increasingly thinner detachments were sent to the annual summer camps at
Aldershot and on Salisbury Plain'.[91]

Overall it is difficult to ascertain the extent of adolescent involvement in the various youth groups during the 1920s and 1930s. The
McNair Report estimated that only 30 per cent of those aged fourteen
to twenty who had left full-time education were attached to any youth
group prior to the outbreak of the Second World War.[92] This estimate
has never been challenged, but alternative evidence appears to indicate
that McNair may well have been somewhat over optimistic. Cameron
found in his survey of unemployed male working-class youth that:[93]

In Cardiff 18%, and in Glasgow 38% of the men in their earlier years
had belonged to one Youth Organisation or another, but only 5% of
the whole sample had carried their membership into the senior section
of an Organisation.

Given that the majority of the members in all voluntary youth were under fourteen it is possible that many of the adolescents in the survey carried out by Cameron had left the organizations to which they had been affiliated before they were fourteen. Probably more indicative of the level of involvement by young people in youth organizations is the raw data on group membership collected by Morgan in 1938,[94] these give an overall affiliation rate of 15.8 per cent. The figure makes no allowance for dual membership and unlike McNair's estimate includes those in the fourteen to twenty age range who are still in full-time education. It seems safe to assume the McNair Report did not underestimate the impact of the various youth organizations, and may well have erred on the side of optimism, and that they were despite all their efforts succeeding in meeting the needs of only a minority of the potential clients.

Certain of the organizations operating before 1914 appear to have found it increasingly difficult to adjust to the changing environment they encountered in the 1920s and 1930s. They were, according to Milson, beginning to 'pass to a defensive stage of self-preservation',[95] which at times encouraged them to adopt an almost 'Blimpish pose' in their attitude towards the contemporary world. For example, Baden-Powell in 1929 juxtaposed cinema stars, Test Matches, Cup Finals, and murders, condemning them all as symbolic of an 'interest in false values', and in the following year the NABC recorded its 'vigorous opposition' to commercialized sport, and equated the cinema with the street corner. At their worst, attitudes such as these justified a certain arrogance which bolstered a number of self-appointed leaders in their role as moral arbiters who should, in the words of one leader working during this period, act as 'shop-windows through which young people can see and admire all that is good and worthwhile'.[96]

A number of youth workers, perhaps not surprisingly, saw in the new youth movements being built in Fascist Italy, Nazi Germany and Communist Russia, a model of what might be achieved given adequate resources and backing. Disturbing comparisons began to be drawn between the youth of depressed Britain and their counterparts in Italy and Germany.[97]

> The Germans and Italians are giving their boys a concrete ideal, a challenge to be fit for their country's sake. The martial which they extol, Englishmen deprecate, hoping that if British boys are not warlike there will be no more war . . . . It may be said that we are presenting our boys with a higher ideal than my-country-right-or-wrong-patriotism . . . and that British boys of today can be fired by the highest collective enthusiasms for the world. Well – perhaps they can. None the less, it may be that young Germans and young Italians

have now a better chance of saving their souls alive than young Englishmen, simply because they are presented with attainable ideals and called upon for practical loyalty.

Eager's remarks published in 'The Boy', the official journal of the NABC, caused considerable controversy, particularly as they were accompanied by 'enthusiastic' reports of the facilities available for young people in the fascist states. For many years the Boys' Club Movement had had strong links with the Jewish boys' clubs that operated in many urban areas and in particular in London, and two nationally prominent members of the NABC, George Lotringa and Basil Henriques, were also Jewish, so any support for the allies of Mosley was certain to arouse hostility in certain quarters. While Jewish shopkeepers and householders in the East End were reporting increasingly 'frenzied victimisation',[98] the London Federation of Boys' Clubs saw fit to invite on a fraternal visit fifteen leaders of the Hitler Jugend. On a more positive level Lotringa as a counter to the spread of anti-semitism opened the first mixed Jewish and Christian boys' club, operating in Bethnal Green; it was soon adjudged a success, but it none the less aroused a certain measure of hostility amongst other leaders operating in the London area. Over fifteen years after Lotringa first removed the religious barriers to membership in his own club Eager still found it relevant to question the wisdom of his policy.[99]

> Common membership without a common religious basis and social tradition lacks moral justification. Inquiring adolescence needs definite answers to its spiritual and moral questions. It is not helped by the theory that one religion is as good as another.

This debate has now become of largely historical interest as all boys' and girls' clubs, statutory and grant-aided provision and the majority of church sponsored groups now operate an 'open-door' policy, but during the period prior to the outbreak of the Second World War it was a source of often bitter controversy.[100]

Improving the physique of the nation

During the 1930s many youth groups began increasingly to concern themselves with the promotion of physical fitness amongst their members. According to Dawes:[101]

> if the pages of 'The Boy' are anything to go by the National Associ- ation of Boys' Clubs was becoming obsessed with physical fitness

(idealised portraits of muscular athletes, naked statutory and bronzes, for boys performing gym and P.T. appear in issue after issue).

As noted earlier this concern found expression in the comparisons that were being drawn between the physical condition of most British youth and that enjoyed by many of their contemporaries in a number of continental countries. A number of reports appeared which seemed to indicate that this concern was well founded,[102] however it is important to note that overall the situation was improving, as Stevenson notes: 'the health of the average Briton was much improved by the inter-war period on what it had been in the past.'[103]

By 1935 Government concern over the physical condition of many young men, particularly those living in the depressed areas, led to the opening of junior transfer centres. The Ministry of Labour funded these centres which were operated by the YMCA[104] where boys who were selected were sent for periods of between eight to ten weeks to enjoy a healthy outdoor life and a well-balanced diet. The three junior transfer centres were supplemented by 'reconditioning camps' financed and operated in the same way as the junior transfer centres, but these only ran during the summer months and offered shorter courses of usually four weeks duration. By 1938 over 3,000 boys had completed a residential period at one of the camps as a direct consequence of the Ministry of Labour grant-aid, however these centres and camps could not hope to radically alter the health status of all but a tiny proportion of the adolescent population.

In November 1936 *The Times* called for 'a great national effort to improve the physique of the Nation'[105] and in the same year it was decided to devote the greatest part of the fund set up in memory of George V to the opening of playing fields to help working class boys keep fit.[106] The growing concern expressed in the media and amongst government spokesmen regarding the physical fitness of the adolescent was to an extent related to the deteriorating international situation. Certainly in military circles it could not have been forgotten that during the First World War 'only one in three conscripts was fit enough to join the forces'[107] particularly as the British Army Council's report for 1933 revealed the following:[108]

During the year 95,270 men and lads offered themselves as recruits to the British Army. 23,582 were rejected on sight, they were so obviously unfit. 71,688 were served with notice papers for a medical test. Out of that number 66,429 were rejected, leaving only 28,841 passing the test.

The drive to improve the health status of the young was not merely a spin-off from the growing threat of a new European war, it was also a reflection of much wider social phenomenon. For during the late 1920s and the 1930s,[109]

> hiking and rambling became almost a national mania ... epitomising the faith which many people had in fresh air and healthy, physical exertion as a positive force for betterment in an often depressing economic climate ... the 'keep-fit' boom, which expressed itself in walking, cycling, sunbathing and sports of every kind. Organisations such as the Women's League of Health and Beauty, which had 16,000 members by 1939, did much to popularise the new cult.

'Fitness' in fact appears to have acquired in some circles a much wider significance. The NABC in 1930 proclaimed 'Fitness' as its aim, and explains:[110]

> The word 'Fitness' embodies most tersely what a club aims at producing and developing in all its members. To every boy with an inclination towards athletics it stands for a high physical ideal. To a club it must mean the fitness of the whole boy for complete manhood.
>
> Fitness, then, in the sense of all-round fitness for the duties and pleasures of life, becomes an epitome of the teaching which all the activities of a club must convey .... With equal simplicity it lends itself to interpretation in its physical, mental and moral aspects ....
> If it is possible to crystallize the practice and ideals of the clubs into a single word, that word is 'fitness'. But it must be fully interpreted. So interpreted and so understood, it might be gloriously inscribed on the banner under which every club-boy would fight the battles of adolescence and win his way to manhood.

It was attitudes such as this which helped to inspire and sustain the 'Keep-Fit' movement and helped to give it a deeper meaning than might be at first apparent.

Perhaps the most successful movement to emerge from the 'Keep-Fit' period was the Youth Hostel Association (YHA) which opened its first hostel in Winchester in 1930 and within ten years had established a chain of over 400 and acquired over 100,000 members.[111] Although the Ramblers' Association founded shortly after the YHA like its predecessor attracted many younger members, neither they or the numerous other 'keep-fit' and health groups which flourished during this period[112] catered exclusively for adolescents, and it would be misleading to describe them as youth work agencies except in the most general terms.

In late 1937 Parliament responding to public pressure passed the 'Physical Training and Recreation Act', which was designed to encourage both local authority and voluntary initiatives that would contribute towards raising the level of national fitness. Local Area Fitness Councils were set up and were empowered to levy a rate to ensure that adequate funds were available for among other things 'the provision of facilities to assist in the maintenance of the physical well-being of young people'. Under Clause 6 of the Act, which was an amendment to Section 86 of the 1921 Education Act, LEAs were permitted to maintain and construct centres for 'athletic, social or educational objects relating to the needs of the young person', which was interpreted to mean that the LEAs were now at liberty to begin operating their own youth centres. The National Fitness Council, set up by the Act, confirmed this by making grants to both voluntary and statutory agencies towards the building costs of youth centres; they were usually in the region of fifty per cent and these were even extended to help with maintenance costs in special circumstances.[113] The Act appears, according to Morgan, to have failed to make any substantial impact in those areas 'in which there is much poverty and which generally are most in need of facilities'[114] for basically it offered aid to those who were capable of helping themselves. Before the effectiveness of the legislation and the various fitness councils could be adequately gauged or amended to increase their efficiency the Second World War broke out, and with it emerged the need for a more direct governmental intervention in the youth work sphere than had hitherto been the accepted norm.

The Second World War

Within two months of the outbreak of war the Government had prepared Circular 1486. This was in the words of Kenneth Lindsay, the Junior Education Minister responsible for drafting it, designed to show that:[115]

> concern is not primarily with delinquency as in 1916, nor with
> nation fitness, as in 1937, but is with the positive all-round develop-
> ment of three million British youths, mostly young workers between
> the ages of 14 and 21. We are in fact adding a fourth province to the
> education service of this country. Primary, secondary and adult edu-
> cation, each has a long and distinguished history, and it is interesting
> to remember that they all started from voluntary effort.

In essence the Circular entitled 'In the Service of Youth' did little more than place a legal obligation on LEAs to take all necessary steps 'to ascertain local gaps and decide where assistance could best be given'. Despite Archbishop Temple's announcement that Circular 1486 marked 'the beginning of an epoch', it really produced very little in way of LEA involvement and the Government was very rapidly obliged to replace it with a far more explicit and directive document.

Circular 1516 followed 1486 in early 1940 and was sub-titled 'The Challenge of Youth'. This laid out in some detail the aims of the 'new' service and proposed the boundaries and future scope of LEA involvement. The Circular instructed LEAs to consider ways in which they might build a service able to 'develop the whole personality of boys and girls to enable them to take their place as full members of a free community'.[116]

Despite their good intentions the Circulars issued in 1939 and 1940 failed to achieve the impact desired by the Government and in consequence they were in turn supplanted by a fare more comprehensive piece of legislation. First announced during the debate on the 1942 National Service Act its purpose, according to the Prime Minister, was to 'ensure that our boys do not run loose during this time of stress'.[117] Published as Board of Education Circular 1577 it required all boys and girls aged sixteen and seventeen to register with their LEA, who were then to advise them as to the ways in which their leisure might be most wisely spent and the opportunities existing within their area for young people to help in the war effort on a voluntary basis. The scheme was not however an unqualified success:[118]

> Attendance at the interview was not compulsory. The initial success of this measure rapidly diminished. The number attending for interview varied between 80 per cent in some areas and 25 per cent in others; some committees issued one invitation, others three or four, and some interviewers even called at houses. The decline in attendance at interviews encouraged more and more committees to adopt a coincident system of registration and interviewing, hoping to cash in on the compulsory element of registration. Youth soon found plenty of ways to sabotage this cunning on the part of adults. The constant figure in this scheme was the small number who actually joined an organisation as the result of the interviewing, and it was no surprise to the young people when the scheme was abandoned. Compulsory interviewing was never adopted because it would have destroyed the essential freedom of the Youth Service.

The war period clearly highlighted the problems that would accompany any attempt by the Government to graft an element of compulsion on to an established voluntary system. However, the need for this did not occur. The Youth Service proved flexible enough to meet the exceptional demands placed upon it by the unique conditions of the period. In terms of membership, levels appear to have been reached between 1939 and 1945 that have never subsequently been attained and a number of groups, in particular the service cadet corps, after years of slow decline found themselves over-subscribed. 'The war supplied the purpose'[119] that many had felt to be previously lacking in much youth work and the results were often impressive giving, perhaps for the only time, the concept of partnership outlined in Circular 1516 real substance and meaning. Evans succeeded in capturing some of the excitement of this period in the following passage:[120]

> The war years were a time of rapid expansion when all were bound together by a clear objective. Grant aid was immediately available from many LEAs and from the Board of Education, from whence financial aid flowed for capital expenditure which covered buildings and equipment, and at that time, for maintenance also, and under this category help towards leaders' salaries (full-time) was also forthcoming from central funds. Annual grants from the Board were awarded to the headquarters of National Voluntary Youth organisations for general administration and for the training of leaders which made it possible for field officers to be appointed to expand and develop their work alongside the Youth Officers appointed by the LEAs. There was little or no difficulty in recruiting leaders and helpers, the need to assist young people under wartime conditions appealed to many as an urgent form of community service, and among the many who came forward to offer their services were teachers living away from home owing to evacuation, who welcomed the opportunities to experiment which the youth service offered . . . .
> The 'open' youth club was a popular form of development and many LEAs particularly in the North of England opened civic youth clubs in school buildings on three or more nights in the week which were entirely staffed by part-time paid leaders and helpers, where those in charge, many of whom had no previous experience in youth work, devised programmes of activities which appeared to them to meet the situation and which certainly attracted numbers of young people; those who joined taking little part in running their own clubs.

The expansion of the Youth Service in response to the exceptional demands placed upon it by war-time conditions generated a renewed interest in youth work in many quarters, an interest which was reflected in the preparation of a number of reports which were designed to ensure that the service retained its new found momentum in the post-war period. All parties were now agreed upon the positive benefits to be derived from increased state intervention therefore the debate largely concerned itself with the form which this intervention should take in the future. The first document to discuss this question was published in 1943, prepared by the National Youth Advisory Council,[121] it was entitled 'The Youth Service After the War'. The report came out firmly against the ethos of much of the existing provision and recommended that henceforth available state funds should be concentrated on the all-age community centres that had developed in the 1930s, stressing that:[122]

> It is essential that the Youth Service should so operate as to lead young people onwards towards adult life and not keep them back unduly in the atmosphere and surroundings of adolescence. We therefore do not regard as ideal the separate 'Youth Centre' with the buildings of the day continuation school as its physical nucleus. We do not want to see young people segregated in this way from the community as a whole. Rather we hope that they will use for some of their leisure activities the buildings of the genuine social centres, community centres or civic centres which we expect to be built after the War.

Sections 41 to 53 of the 1944 Education Act were crucial for the Youth Service for they were designed to integrate it into the national educational structure and to formalize many of the practices that had developed on an *ad hoc* basis during the war years. The Act gave notice to all concerned that when the constraints of the war economy had been removed the Government intended to become a full and active partner in the provision of facilities for youth work, and that it was no longer willing to entrust the social education of large sections of the adolescent population solely to the existing voluntary organizations staffed overwhelmingly by well-meaning amateurs. The principle of state intervention first mooted in the 1918 and 1921 Education Acts was both extended and made more explicit. The Butler Act brought to an end the voluntary principle which had allowed LEAs to opt out of involvement in youth work, henceforth it was to be no longer an optional but a statutory duty on the part[123]

> of every local education authority to secure the provision for their area of adequate facilities for further education . . . (including) . . .

leisure time occupation . . . for any person over compulsory school age who is able and willing to profit by the facilities provided for that purpose . . . (and) . . . to secure that the facilities for primary and secondary and further education provided for their area include adequate facilities for recreation and social training . . . (having) regard to the expediency of co-operation with any voluntary societies or bodies whose objects include the provision of facilities or the organisation of activities of a similar character.

For large-scale local authority intervention to become a reality, and in particular to enable the LEAs to intervene in those areas where the voluntary organizations were at their weakest, it was essential that an adequate supply of trained full-time staff should become available. The Government therefore appointed the McNair Committee to look into the question of the training and remuneration of community centre wardens and youth leaders. The McNair Report estimated that the post-war Youth Service would require at the minimum 'between 5,000 and 6,000 full-time workers'.[124] These would be highly professional, and be recruited from the widest possible variety of backgrounds. They would be on average older than trainee teachers when they were initially recruited having previously been employed in industry or commerce before commencing their youth leadership training. Partly with this in mind McNair opted for an independent training scheme: 'We do not think that training for youth leadership should be attempted within the course designed to train teachers and other kinds of social worker.'[125]

The initial response of the Government to the McNair Report was favourable and funds were made available for several universities to set up courses which it was envisaged would be capable of meeting the predicted demand for qualified staff. By 1953 all but one of the five courses that had eventually begun to recruit students had ceased operating apparently owing to a lack of suitably qualified applicants.[126]

Two further committees were appointed by the Ministry of Education to examine questions relating to the staffing of the youth and community services. Both published reports with the identical title, 'The Report of the Committee on the Recruitment, Training and Conditions of Service of Youth Leaders and Community Centre Wardens'. The first of these panels was known as the Jackson Committee and it published its findings in 1949. It called for urgent Government action to increase the number and quality of recruits and the linking of their training and remuneration to that of school teachers, for both groups the report concluded 'should be regarded as branches of one common service'. This second recommendation was 'met by a storm of protest',[127] and a second committee was appointed in 1950. Known as the Fletcher Committee, it largely endorsed the proposals of the earlier McNair Report, recommending not only separate training for youth leaders and community centre wardens from that given to school teachers, but also the adoption of policies that would ensure the recruitment of mature students 'from industry and social work as well as from teaching'.

The end result of all these deliberations amounted to very little. Even as the committees were meeting courses closed down[128] which were not replaced, and as one commentator has noted 'from the early 1950s to the end of the decade, relatively few full-time youth leaders were trained in this country'.[129]

Post-war: voluntary – statutory partnership

Despite the abundant good will which the Youth Service had acquired from its contribution to the war effort and the publication of an unprecedented number of reports on the future development and staffing of the service, the immediate post-war years were to set the seal on a decade and a half of slow, unremitting decline that was only finally reversed by the injection of capital which followed the publication of the Albemarle Report in 1960. It was particularly unfortunate that the opportunity to construct a real partnership between the voluntary and statutory sectors was dissipated by the lack of commitment to youth work on the part of the Government and many LEAs. The voluntary organizations in 1945 were strong enough to play a full and equal part, which they were arguably not by 1960, in the partnership proposed by Circular 1516 and reiterated in the 1944 Education Act, and equally important, the experience of co-operating with the statutory agencies during the war years had dispelled any lingering doubts they may have had, that co-operation would inevitably lead to their absorption in a monolithic state controlled youth service. The voluntary organizations by the end of the 1940s appear to have been not only convinced of the value of partnership but also anxious to extend it, as Lord Aberdare, the Chairman of the NABC, noted in 1947:[130]

> Since 1939, when the Board of Education asked local education authorities to set up youth committees the state has assumed an ever-increasing responsibility for the welfare of young people. In some areas voluntary organisations were encouraged and supported by local authorities, but in other areas they set up and controlled

their own recreational institutes, without showing any desire to co-operate with voluntary clubs. The Ministry, recognising the dangers of a state controlled uniformity and regimentation in the field of youth service, has urged the local authorities to pursue a policy of partnership with the voluntary organisations . . . . The grant aid which the Ministry has placed at the disposal of the N.A.B.C. has made possible developments which would otherwise have been impossible; there can be no doubt that the full extension of such a partnership, so that it operates between the N.A.B.C.'s Country Association and the local education authorities would do much to further the growth of boys' clubs.

The optimism of Lord Aberdare concerning the future of the Youth Service was shared by the Standing Conference of National Voluntary Youth Organizations (SCNVYO) who following their conference in 1945 published a document entitled 'Partnership in the Service of Youth'. This envisaged not only building upon the successes of the preceding five years but also seizing the opportunity presented by the 1944 Education Act to once more shift the emphasis of youth work:[131]

The voluntary organisations rejoice in the improved educational opportunities for all young people and are planning to make a parallel advance in leisure time education to keep pace with the school.

The very fact that their members will, in coming years, be better educated, be better nourished, and longer under school discipline, will relieve them of much they had to do in the past to remedy deficiencies in culture and character, and enable them properly to concentrate on teaching the art of using leisure time – of using it for the upbuilding of character, at once strengthened by self-discipline and enriched by the exercise of a free initiative.

These hopes were in the main to be short-lived. The planned raising of the school-leaving age to sixteen was to be delayed for nearly twenty years and the introduction of a national network of county colleges to cater for the post-school education of the adolescent has never materialized. The training schemes designed to provide an influx of skilled professional youth leaders into youth work faltered and then failed partly through a lack of finance, but also due to a failure on the part of a contracting Youth Service to attract the right calibre of trainees. The economic difficulties of the post-war years also meant that the 1945 level of Government expenditure on youth provision was halved in 1946 and had still not recovered by 1951 when Sir John Maud the then Permanent Secretary of the Ministry of Education warned the Youth Service 'that the realistic assumption to make is that it is going to be difficult to maintain the amount of public money which is at present flowing, whether from central government or from local government, into the Youth Service.'[132]

In 1951 the King George's Jubilee Trust called a two-day conference at Ashridge to debate the 'Youth Service of Tomorrow'. By then it was apparent that the expansion that had seemed a real possibility in the early and mid-1940s was not going to take place. Maud informed the conference, made up of representatives of both voluntary organizations and local authorities that the Youth Service had 'had a raw deal' and should not hope for a better one in the near future.[133] The report of the conference makes somewhat sombre reading; it talks of declining membership[134] and the seemingly intractable problems 'of not enough money, not enough buildings, and too few real people as leaders, a policy of fewer organisations and fewer organisers and administrators.'[135] The conference made a number of recommendations, calling in particular for increased Government investment in the Youth Service and the introduction of training schemes for both full and part-time leaders.[136] It also agreed upon a statement:[137]

> That all Youth Work should be based on the principle that national well-being requires that there should be preserved or born a genuinely Christian civilisation in which belief in God sets the tone for Society and that to this end opportunities should be made available to all youth groups for the development of religious faith.

The conference, apart from agreeing upon a common statement of intent, appears to have achieved very little, for it failed to arrest the decline in the fortunes of the Youth Service. No more Government or local authority funds became available, and no policy on the recruitment of full-time staff came into operation that might halt the net outflow of professional leaders that was taking place annually. This was a particularly disturbing trend. In 1948 Younghusband had estimated that there were probably 1,800 full-time paid leaders;[138] by 1951 Kuenstler put the figure at 1,500,[139] and by 1953 it stood at 825[140] and continued falling to around 700 in 1960.[141] It was a decline that was in no way compensated for by an expansion in the recruitment of part-time paid leaders whose ranks increased only slightly from 4,500 in 1951[142] to 4,600 in 1959.[143]

By 1955 the problems of the Youth Service had reached such a pitch that a King George Jubilee Trust working party under the Chairmanship of J.F. Wolfenden could declare that:[144]

> the Youth Service is at the parting of the ways. The nation must decide, and express its decision through its representatives and through the administrators who act on their behalf the plain question whether it wishes the Youth Service, and all that it stands for, to survive and prosper, or whether it is prepared to see it, and all that it can provide for our young people, shrink away and perish.

Lord Aberdare, who had been so confident regarding the future of the Youth Service in 1947, endorsed the comments of Sir John Wolfenden and entitled his address to the 1956 annual conference of the NABC 'The Youth Service is in Grave Danger' and the delegates decided that his warning should be circulated to all members of both Houses of Parliament in the hope that they might intercede on its behalf. No sector of youth work appears to have escaped the general malaise. Fyvel in noting that 'the Scout movement has probably had its day among boys and girls over thirteen and fourteen'[145] was probably speaking for all the long established uniformed groups. Certainly Thomas and Perry found in their survey carried out in 1975 that over 50 per cent of the Scouts, Guides, Boys' Brigade and Girls' Brigade were under thirteen and fewer than 8 per cent were aged sixteen and over.[146]

The Albemarle Committee were probably not unduly exaggerating when they talked of the Youth Service in 1959 as being in 'a state of acute depression . . . dying on its feet'.[147] Voluntarism by the close of the 1950s appeared to have run its course and the Youth Service to be facing a future that depended increasingly upon the willingness of central and local government to lend both moral and financial support.

2   The Albemarle years

The Albemarle Committee was to prove an organizational and intellectual watershed for the Youth Service. The full force of its impact has far from evaporated with the passing of time and as Eggleston discovered in his recent survey of youth workers, the Albemarle Report 'remains the most convenient and certainly the most reliable guide to the "official" ideology and values of the service.'[1] For that reason, if for no other, it seems essential nearly eighteen years after its initial publication, to examine both its background and findings.

The Albemarle Committee was created by a Minister of Education who could not have been unaware that he was in the near future likely to be subjected to considerable criticism concerning his department's handling of its responsibilities apropos the Youth Service. The announcement that the Government was setting up a Committee chaired by Lady Albemarle to review the Youth Service's role was a timely one, coming as it did only a matter of days prior to the start of a scheduled debate in the Commons on the future of the service.

Severe criticism had earlier been levelled at the Ministry of Education concerning its approach to youth work. The Select Committee on Government Estimates, an influential back bench parliamentary body, had in an overwhelmingly critical review noted that it was[2]

> not satisfied that the Ministry of Education was properly exercising its responsibility for the money spent. The impression gained from the Inquiry is that the Ministry is little interested in the present state of the service and apathetic about its future. Your Committee considers that this apathy is having a deeply discouraging effect on the valuable work done for the service – much of it voluntary and unpaid.

The comments of the MPs who constituted the Select Committee did not go unnoticed, and in particular they led to both a series of questions in the House and to a well publicized debate in the House of Lords[3] which was opened by Lord Pakenham who quoted at length from the Report.

The parliamentary activity although important should however be viewed in a much wider context. At one level it reflected the concern expressed in the 1955 Report 'Citizens of Tomorrow'[4] and echoed in the statements of many spokesmen of the voluntary organizations, over the declining impact of the Youth Service and its ailing finances; at another level it coincided with a more general debate fostered by press[5] and television on adolescent and juvenile delinquency and other aspects of what might be loosely termed teenage culture. Certainly a great deal of the popular literature of this period concerning the behaviour of adolescents often bordered on the alarmist and helped to convey an impression that Britain was in the grip of 'a wave of youthful lawlessness, expressed both in mob hooliganism and, more seriously, in a steady rise of juvenile crime figures.'[6]

The real depth of public concern is obviously difficult to gauge due to the often ambivalent role of the press. For example, the Daily Mirror was busily manipulating between late 1958 and early 1959 a campaign for the voluntary surrender of weapons by the members of teenage gangs and orchestrating public support for a Private Members' Bill to prohibit the sale and possession of flick-knives whilst it was simultaneously extracting the maximum coverage from any manifestation of 'teenage violence'. Certainly subsequent research[7] has raised many questions concerning the motivation and role of the press in its handling of news relating to adolescent delinquency; however by the late 1950s whatever the precise role of the press and the true extent of public concern, the Home Office had reached the conclusion that the problem was serious enough to warrant a major governmental intervention.

In 1959 the Home Secretary called 'a conference at the highest level on the prevention of delinquency'[8] and published a White Paper[9] outlining a substantial prison building programme that laid special emphasis upon the treatment of young offenders. Funds were to be made available for the construction of eight Borstals and for a further eight of the new Detention Centres which were designed to 'administer a short sharp shock' to the more recalcitrant young offenders. The courts were also strengthened, and to enable them to deal with the more peripheral members of the 'teenage gangs' the offence of 'causing an affray' was resurrected after decades of legal redundancy. The cumulative effect of the media campaigns, legislative enactments and public debate was that, correctly or not, 'by 1960 . . . British public opinion had woken up to the existence of an alarming streak of violence among a section of its youth.'[10]

A great deal of the academic response to this 'youth problem' tended to concentrate upon the task of isolating and quantifying the new and distinctive characteristics of the 'teenage culture'. Whether examining patterns of adolescent consumption,[11] peer group behaviour,[12] cultural characteristics of the teenage life-style[13] or role conflict within the educational environment,[14] the studies tended to share a common reference point in Parsons definition of youth as being 'more or less irresponsible', in contrast to the responsibility essential for performing adult roles. It was an attitude which manifested itself, according to Parsons, in 'a strong tendency to repudiate interest in adult things and to feel at least a certain recalcitrance to the pressure of adult expectations and discipline.'[15]

The debates concerning the veracity and value of this analysis, and of the welter of research that it underpinned, are not central to this study, what is however important is the need to recognize that it had a substantial impact in lending support to the theory that a distinctive and recognizable adolescent life-style was feasible and was emerging as a by-product of the affluence engendered by the post-war economic boom.[16] A not atypical rendition of this thesis, which saw a growing alienation amongst adolescents from the norms of established adult society as an almost inevitable corollary of structural changes in the industrial and educational systems and the growth of technology is presented by Watson who saw[17]

> the emergence of a category of adolescents with special needs and duties is a consequence of a number of allied social processes, first the occupational and social diversity found in industrial societies which are subject to rapid technical and social changes, second the need for prolonged vocational and cultural education that will enable young people to cope with this diversity, and third the trend towards earlier physical maturity brought about by higher standards of living and improved medical care . . . . As a result, physiological maturity and social maturity are tending to become increasingly out of phase, for the social need for a high level of literate and technical education delays the achievement of adult occupation and statuses. This is the period of adolescence.

Coleman, writing admittedly from an American standpoint, goes even further than Watson in postulating that these societal pressures have created for the teenager 'distinct adolescent social systems', that embrace a way of life which is not only different from but largely opposed to that of the adult world and its value system. He maintains that this separation derives largely from the increasing length of the school experience in modern society and the growing breadth of that experience, which ensure that the teenager is[18] cut off from the rest of society, forced inwards towards his own age group, made to carry out his whole social life with others of his own age group. With his fellows he comes to constitute a small society, one that has most of its main interactions with itself and maintains only a few threads of connection with the outside adult society . . . to put it simply these young people speak a different language. What is more relevant to the present point, the language they speak is becoming more and more different.

At a micro level Abrams, in monitoring the consumer spending patterns of the 'new' affluent teenagers, both borrowed from and lent support to the constructs of such writers as Watson and Coleman. Abrams claimed to have isolated patterns of 'distinctive teenage spending for distinctive teenage ends in a distinctive teenage world', wherein, 'the quite large amount of money at the disposal of Britain's average teenager is spent mainly on dressing up in order to impress other teenagers and on goods which form the nexus of teenage gregariousness outside the home.'[19] It was a phenomenon that Abrams was to subsequently stress reflected few 'class differences in income and expenditure'.[20] In emphasizing the classlessness in patterns of teenage consumption Abrams places his study in direct lineage to the work of writers such as Dahrendorf, Crosland and Bell,[21] possessing as it does an ideological perspective that fits neatly into the niche occupied by the embourgeoisement thesis which envisaged the gradual erosion of class differentials and conflict before the rolling tide of affluence and consumerism.

In similar vein much of the early literature that became known as the 'sociology of youth' tended to obscure, not only class, but also racial and ethnic variations amongst young people by over-emphasizing the influence and universality of a distinctive teenage culture.[22] All too often adolescents came to be viewed as a homogeneous entity. In perhaps its most extreme form this viewpoint aligned itself with McLuhan's belief that all adolescents in the western industrialized nations had so distanced themselves from adult norms and values that it was possible to consider that 'All our teenagers are now tribal. That is, they recognise their total involvement in the human family regardless of their personal goals or backgrounds.'[23] To view the child as a member of a unique generation set apart from their parents by the experience of a childhood spent in a new electronic environment; the TV child that expects 'involvement and doesn't want a specialist job in the future. He does want a *role* and deep commitment to his society. Unbridled and misunderstood' (emphasis in original).[24]

This cult of youth[25] which attracted so much journalistic and academic interest during the 1950s and 1960s now seems to have lost its impetus. The debate concerning the value of a separate sociology of youth remains,[26] but the more extreme positions adopted by many of the earlier protagonists seem to have been discredited by much subsequent research,[27] which has highlighted the extent to which young and old share attitudes and norms rather than in exaggerating the often marginal generational differences that generate conflict.[28] The result has been reflected in a more measured and careful analysis of teenage culture, which, as Cohen points out, shows it to be far from the homogeneous entity that many claimed it to be, for[29]

> although its artefacts might be blandly classless, it is highly stratified along class, regional, educational and other lines. Moreover, since its creation in the fifties, a mainstream of teenage entertainment culture has been conformist in character, and conspicuous for its passivity and continuity with adults.

Much of the mythology surrounding teenage culture has been shed revealing it to be like most features of adolescent life 'a reverberation of adult life'.[30]

In the period prior to the 'rediscovery' of poverty by writers such as Harrington in the USA and Abel-Smith and Townsend in Britain, the political consensus embodied in 'Butskellism' pervaded much of the political arena. In such a climate the theories of Watson, Coleman *et al.*, helped to provide an acceptable functionalist explanation, for what to many observers seemed almost inexplicable, namely why should certain groups of young people exhibit the symptoms of alienation, and delinquency rates rise when the worst aspects of multiple deprivation which it was assumed had spawned such behaviour patterns in the 'bad old days' had been all but eliminated by the welfare state. Some commentators, such as the Chairman of the Metropolitan Juvenile Court, assumed that if poverty was no longer the root cause of teenage crime then somehow affluence must be. Writing in 1961 he argued, 'Poverty is no longer a major cause of crime. I believe that today a major cause is the availability of too many material benefits in return for too little effort.'[31] Of course, if affluence *per se* is a cause of juvenile delinquency then presumably the magistrate would have found his court dealing with a disproportionately high percentage of young persons drawn from the wealthier classes, which was patently not the case. Given the unquestioning belief held by many commentators in the efficacy of the 'welfare state' the assumption that affluence was an important and growing cause of crime amongst adolescents was perhaps understand-able. However, all too often this analysis degenerated into a belief that somehow working-class youngsters were in many cases emotionally and temperamentally ill-equipped to handle affluence, and would be better off with less rather than more money in their pockets.[32] A rising stan-dard of living thus came to be seen as a mixed blessing, that both reduced the dangers of class conflict, but in so doing upset the 'natural order of things', and it was this belief which[33]

> touched the delicate and ambivalent nerves through which post-war
> social change in Britain was experienced . . . messages about 'never
> having it so good' were ambivalent in that some people were having
> it too good too quickly . . . resentment and jealousy were easily
> directed at the young, if only because of their increased spending
> power and sexual freedom. When this was combined with a too
> often flouting of the work and leisure ethic and the (as yet) uncer-
> tain threats associated with drug-taking, something more than the
> image of a peaceful Bank Holiday at the sea was being shattered.

The changes in living standards were to emerge on subsequent closer examination as largely ones of style rather than of essence, for little real re-distribution of wealth had taken place following the onset of the 1950s. Indeed by 1960 it has been argued that the small gains made by the lower-paid and welfare recipients relative to the rest of the popula-tion during the immediate post-war period, 1945–51, were fast evapor-ating.[34] The illusion of fundamental change was, it appears, far more the result of an acceleration in the process of 'Stratified Diffusion';[35] brought about by the abandonment of rationing and controls combined with the skilful orchestration of consumer booms that served the dual function of injecting buoyancy into the economy and simultaneously boosting the electoral prospects of the incumbent government,[36] than was possibly apparent at the time. The 1950s and 1960s were decades when affluence for all seemed a real possibility, a view that was based upon a confident belief, widely held,[37]

> that a new society was emerging, that with properly run government,
> prosperity and expansion were assured. Academics discussed the
> post-industrial and affluent societies. Television programmes began
> to cover the so-called 'leisure problem'. Economists were cheery
> optimistic men.

This air of sanguine consensus helped to lend credibility to a belief that many long-standing social problems were being effectively tackled or had even been already solved. It was argued, for example, that the old class divisions no longer had any real meaning, as one Conservative Minister put it, 'In Britain today every single one of us belongs to the working classes.'[38] This remark attracted wide publicity and only a little incredulity when it was made.

Those who questioned this vision of a new Britain, united and class-less, and growing every more so by the hour, either by word or deed, tended to be consigned to the intellectual or social periphery. Left-wing politicians and theorists who challenged the 'quite unusual degree of political relaxation and consensus',[39] were labelled, if noticed, old-fashioned class warriors, by a process that Thompson has termed 'intel-lectual McCarthyism', whereby Marxist or neo-Marxist writers were deemed 'so disreputable that they could find little expression outside of Communist publications'.[40] Shop stewards became both a media joke and objects of derision, castigated by politicians, industrialists and even their own union leaders as latter-day Luddites fighting causes long since won. Teddy-boys, mods and rockers, beatniks and drop-outs were viewed with similar disdain as anti-social deviants, objects of both con-tempt and fear, caricatured in the media, often portrayed in the world of B-films and TV plays as psychopaths[41] and in cartoons as *lumpen* Neanderthals. In such a climate all too often alienated youth became for many little more than the bored, mindless, nihilistic outcasts of a pampered generation.[42] It was an evaluation of teenage culture that by its own internal logic precluded *a priori* any recognition of the possibility that such patterns of behaviour might represent mere symptoms of a far deeper malaise rooted within society itself.[43]

Such attitudes certainly help to explain the often exasperated, puzzled tones of the Albemarle Report when it asks why those 'young people enjoying the first class housing . . . of the new housing estates and blocks of flats'[44] should still present a 'problem'. One response, particularly relevant to the Youth Service was to define the problem as being partly one of leadership. Albemarle talks of a 'bragging lawless' element that offers the young a dangerous example and whom it was hoped could be negated by youth workers trained and equipped to offer the young a 'constructive alternative' consisting of 'Association, Training and Challenge'.[45]

Goffman ascribes social power to those who control 'the definition of the situation'.[46] In the context of the youth 'problem' of the1950s and the early 1960s, this meant that the youth were viewed as deviating from a well-defined normality and solutions were overwhelmingly seen in terms of social engineering and individual pathology. This definition however created its own 'problems', as Eysenck recognized in an article which pressed the case for social conditioning:[47]

> The problem to be discussed is: how can we engineer a social consent which will make people behave in a socially adapted, law-abiding fashion, which will not lead to a breakdown of the intricately inter-woven fabric of social life? Clearly we are failing to do this: the ever-increasing number of unofficial strikes, the ever-increasing statistics of crime of all sorts, the general alienation on which so many writers have commented, are voluble witnesses to this statement. The psychologist would answer that what was clearly required was a technology of consent – that is, a generally applicable method of inculcating suitable habits of socialised conduct into the citizens (and particularly the future citizens) of the country.

A factor which gave added weight to the social control element of the debate relating to the value of youth work intervention was in part a direct consequence of the mounting pressure being exerted upon the Government to abandon conscription. In addition to the electoral bene-fit that it was widely held would accrue to the party responsible for bringing National Service to an end, powerful economic arguments were put forward in favour of abolition. It was argued that economic expan-sion was being retarded by a labour shortage, and in respect of this problem only two short-term solutions appeared open to the Govern-ment. One entailed the encouragement of further immigration; the other, admittedly of far more limited potential, but politically more acceptable was to release on to the labour market the 200,000-plus National Servicemen.

Conscription was, however, in certain quarters, held to be beneficial for both society as a whole, and for the individual conscript, for as one Albemarle witness explained, 'it developed not only physical activities, but also self-reliance and the capacity to work in a group and to accept organised discipline for a common purpose.'[48] Whatever the rights or wrongs of this argument, it must be set against the belief that National Service often seriously disrupted the full- and part-time educa-tion and training of many young men, and also inflicted considerable financial hardship upon others who were either already married or preparing for marriage. Leaving aside the arguments for and against retention, the cessation of National Service would release around a quarter of a million males aged between eighteen and twenty-three back into the mainstream of civilian life.[49] Freed from the constraints of a military regime many commentators feared that in addition to placing a greater strain upon the already over-stretched youth and further education facilities this group would exacerbate the ever-worsening crime figures by remaining within peer groups from which they had previously been removed at eighteen. Subsequent research[50] has shown a sharp decline in delinquency rates amongst young males following a peak at the ages of sixteen and seventeen, in 1958 however it was a realistic assumption that this decline was in some way related to conscription rather than to more obscure factors.

In the light of the events of the preceding months and years and the imminent end to National Service the members of the Albemarle Committee appeared to have felt that they were under considerable pressure to prepare a report within the shortest possible time. This impression of haste is confirmed by an HMI who worked closely with the Committee, who reports that the panel 'recognized the urgency of their task and work started immediately'.[51]

The task at hand was encapsulated for the Committee in its terms of reference, set out by the Minister of Education; it requested that they,[52]

> Review the contribution which the Youth Service of England and Wales can make in assisting young people to play their part in the life of the community, in the light of changing social and industrial conditions and of current trends in other branches of the education service, and to advise according to what priorities best value can be obtained for the money spent.

However, beneath such bland generalities, as Hamilton notes, the Government and the members of the Albemarle Committee shared a common concern regarding the behaviour of large sections of the adolescent population, a concern that meant that from the onset all parties predominately 'saw the problem as one of social control'.[53]

With the benefit of hindsight it is possible to demote those causes for concern as being somewhat premature for 1958 and the preceding decade served as little more than a prelude to what later came to be distinguished as youth culture and its corollary, the so-called adolescent rebellion. For yet to occur were such manifestations of this 'rebellion' as the Beatlemania of the early 1960s, the 'drug explosion' that seemed to emanate from Haight Ashbury in 1967, the Mods and Rocker clashes, the outbreak of 'Paki-bashing' which attracted so much media attention in 1969, the sit-ins, demonstrations and hyper-political activity amongst students *circa* 1968-9, and the ongoing saga of football hooliganism. In comparison to the aforementioned list the decade which pre-dated Albemarle might well register as halcyon days of adolescent tranquillity, broken only by the isolated and sporadic violence of gangs of 'teddy-boys' fighting each other over territory,[54] or ritualistically slashing cinema seats to celebrate the screening of the latest rock and roll film, but that is for the events of the summer of 1958. A matter of months prior to the appointment of the Albemarle Committee the 'youth problem' had taken on a new and potentially terrifying dimension in the form of violent racial conflict. This was admittedly confined in the main to certain urban areas; in 1958 the riots centred on Nottingham and London, and in the latter it was the Notting Hill and Brixton areas that experienced the worst violence, but the intensity of the clashes and the speed with which minor incidents escalated into large-scale confrontations[55] seemed to augur ill for the future. Certainly, the full impact and horror of these outbreaks could not have evaporated from the memories of the Albemarle panel when they assembled, particularly as their early meetings coincided with the appearance in court of a number of youths who had been involved, and who amid a flourish of publicity received exemplary sentences.

The 'problem' youth of the decade preceding 1958 appeared to be almost exclusively drawn from the working class,[56] the 'Teds' convicted after the Notting Hill race riot, for example, were all 'unskilled working class adolescents'.[57] The pre-1958 rebellion, if it can be graced with that epithet, possessed none of the political connotation it was to acquire in later years from groups such as the Yippies[58] and from cult figures such as Dylan.[59] The ad-mix of deviant life-style and radical politics was still nearly a decade away in 1958, even in America where the fusion of the two *circa* 1968 prompted Horowitz and Liebowitz to claim that 'the line between the social deviant and the political marginal is fading. It is rapidly becoming an obsolete distinction.'[60] However superficial and unreal the links between 'radical chic' writers such as Marcuse, Laing and Leary, and the prevalent youth culture of that period it is possible to discern by the end of the 1960s a veneer of politicization and intellectuality that was totally absent during the years prior to Albemarle.[61]

For Albemarle the youth problem was in essence a working-class phenomenon, although given many of the assumptions prevalent at that time regarding the declining significance of class as a social entity it tended not to discuss the 'problem' in those terms. It did, however, recognize that the situation was far from stable when it refers to those 'elements to which adolescents are responding sharply and often in ways which adults find puzzling and shocking.'[62] However, Albemarle all too often lapses into emotive language and wild generalizations concerning young people that cannot but harm its case. For example when it talks of 'bragging lawless teenagers (who hope) that their contemporaries will accept them as stronger than society,'[63] or as in another example, which is in reality an attack upon the moral standards of tens of thousands of young people and which incidentally displays graphically the narrow class perspectives of the panel, maintaining that,[64]

> every teenager in congested areas knows of offences committed in the neighbourhood and not discovered. He hears them boasted about in public places. He knows that a life of crime rarely discovered is possible, and this shakes his faith in the order and dignity of the society in which he lives.

There is no attempt by the Albemarle Report to quantify such statements with hard evidence based upon a modicum of empirical research, so they remain impossible either to validate or to disprove.[65] All the Report succeeds in doing is giving added credibility to what might be at best half truths.

Equally disturbing is the ease and regularity with which the Albemarle Report talks of a 'crime wave amongst the young'. This assertion is supported merely in statistical terms by the presentation of raw data relating to conviction rates for indictable offences committed by young persons aged eight to twenty for 1938 and the years between 1945 and 1958. No analysis is offered, but if it had been it would have shown that whereas in 1945 1.7 per cent of males aged sixteen were convicted of indictable offences by 1958 the figure stood at 2.1 per cent (an increase of 0.4 per cent), while among females of the same age group the growth was in the region of 0.225 per cent. These are hardly figures capable of supporting the term 'crime wave'. Nor does the Report attempt to determine how many of these charges were brought under the Highway Act.[66] Between 1945 and 1958 motor-cycle sales had grown from 150,000 to almost 1,750,000 annually. As young people were the main purchasers of both new and second-hand motor-cycles it is not difficult to see the extent to which they as an age group were at increased legal risk. Indeed the growth in conviction rates in this area alone could largely account for the increase in juvenile crime.

It is not, however, the raw data alone that would have benefited from closer scrutiny and a more open mind, for other less tangible factors can be at work in the definition of a crime wave, as Young shows in his study, 'The Role of the Police as Amplifiers of Deviancy'.[67] The media, political pressure and organizational restructuring within the police can all help to create a 'crime wave'. The definition of a problem by the press[68] for example puts the police under considerable pressure to make arrests, they in consequence transfer resources, thus increasing the detection rate, especially in relation to victimless crime. For example, by setting up a drug squad within an area the police create a body of men and women who must find drug-users in order to justify their role, this inevitably leads to a rise in the crime rate. In the atmosphere prevailing during the mid- and late 1950s it is likely that minor offences committed by teenagers, particularly those wearing a distinctive uniform, i.e. 'teddy-boys', such as rowdiness, drunkenness and horseplay, which in the past might have merely led to a verbal warning from the constable on the beat or an admonishment from a more senior officer, might well, and probably did in many cases, lead to a prosecution. Heussenstamm,[69] in an American context, clearly showed the extent to which the police may be selective as to the social groups they choose to harass and prosecute. In Britain during this period the 'teddy-boys' and 'rockers' with their distinctive modes of dress could not have failed to have attracted the attention of the police in much the same way that Black Panther stickers attracted American police later.

The concentration of the media and the police upon the young deviant had wider implications than the mere containment of crime. It was as Scott points out, part of a much wider educative process whereby the state spells out to the young the parameters of state power, for:[70]

> To contain and control deviance and thereby master it, is to supply fresh and dramatic proof of the enormous powers behind the social order. The visible control of deviance is one of the most effective mechanisms by which a social order can tangibly display its potency. The act of harnessing things which are dangerous helps to revitalise the system by demonstrating to those who live within it just how awesome its powers really are.

The Albemarle Committee along with the Government recognized that the Youth Service had an important role to play as an agency for the control of adolescent deviance. The inherent catch in such a commitment is that it offers a hostage to fortune, whereby the future performance of the Youth Service might be measured against criteria over which it has fundamentally no control and precious little influence.

Generalizations and prognostications regarding both contemporary and future trends in crime, like those relating to demography, appear difficult to make and dangerous to apply. This did not deter the members of the Albemarle panel, who proclaimed that it was possible to 'speak of a new climate of crime and delinquency. We have been made intensely aware of this and we accept the significant public warnings of judges and police chiefs.'[71] Unfortunately the panel do not seriously examine the validity of such public warnings. For 'police chiefs', if they are nothing else, are heads of bureaucratic organizations who often justify their role and the size of the undertaking they control, while legitimizing their actions by stressing the potential dangers of unbridled criminality. They have paradoxically a vested interest in crime, and one of the only legitimate methods they have of increasing the man-power and resources at their disposal is by the creation of a public concern regarding the danger posed by crime. A chillingly simple equation of more crime equals more police equals enhanced status for the police chief begins to emerge; it is in fact arguable that the very foundations of a pluralist system depend upon the Chief Constables, and others in similar positions, making such demands upon public resources. However, within such a system it becomes incumbent upon all parties concerned with broader policy objectives to base these upon the soundest possible data and projections. This the Albemarle Committee did not do. It opted for the easy way out by the collection of hearsay evidence only.

The Albemarle Report is a rushed and ill-prepared document. Its authors at the onset virtually admit this when they write in only the third paragraph:[72]

> we have . . . been meeting in conditions of unusual urgency and with a sense of working against time. As a result we have not undertaken any large scale research projects in what is a very wide field. These can be carried out once the main justification and aims of the Service have been established.

In other words 'we won't bother unduly with facts, we will just get on with planning, fitting reality into our grand design': a recipe for chaos and the wasteful allocation of resources if there ever was one. With a measure of justification, Musgrove came to dismiss the Albemarle Report as 'one of the most disastrous social documents to appear in this country this century . . . which no doubt with the best intentions in the world belittles and humiliates the young.'[73]

The Report was completed in less than twelve months and its main recommendations were accepted on the day of their publication by the Minister of Education, without even the most cursory public, professional or parliamentary debate taking place. Revealingly, an HMI of the period has since written that had such a debate taken place it would have had little effect upon future policy, for even 'while the Committee was still sitting internal arrangements had been made to deal with an expanded service, and a high ranking official with assistants had been put in charge of the administrative work.'[74] The forward planning of the civil servants was not to be disrupted by any particularly startling recommendations from the Committee. In the main these were both safe and predictable, which is hardly surprising if one examines the list of establishment figures drawn from the Youth Service who presented evidence to the panel. As a report on Youth Service development produced by one LEA put it:[75]

> the recommendations of the Albemarle Committee were extensively
> based on the knowledge and experience of youth organisations as
> they existed in the late 1950s, a glance at the organisations which
> submitted evidence will tend to confirm that. It is, therefore, hardly
> surprising if the Youth Service has grown up against this background
> and has, in the process greatly strengthened what we may now call
> the 'orthodox' youth club provision.

Compared with the varied range of witnesses called and the imaginative series of investigative visits undertaken by the subsequent Fairbairn-Milson Committee, Albemarle was very much a pedestrian exercise.

From a total of forty-four the Committee selected its four principal recommendations:

(a) A ten-year development programme for the Youth Service, divided into two stages of five years each. For this period an Advisory Committee of not more than twelve persons to be called the Youth Service Development Council, to be set up.

(b) A generous and imaginative building programme to be set in motion.

(c) The Minister to take steps to increase the existing force of full-time leaders.

(d) A negotiating committee for the salaries and conditions of service of full-time leaders to be set up.

All these were accepted and implemented by the Minister.

The tragedy of the Albemarle Report may well be that it was so uncritically welcomed at the time of its publication. This favourable reception was probably a measure of the weakness of the Youth Service at this juncture, for Albemarle heralded 'the passing of those barren years of the 1950s' and criticism was[76]

> drowned in the noise and clamour to get forward into the new
> decade with the hopes and challenges of a new era, the feeling that
> at least the work which had gone on so patiently and so quietly had

been recognised for what it was – an indispensable part of the country's effort to produce new generations.

The sigh of relief in the Youth Service over the Government's acceptance of Albemarle's policy of expansion rather than of further retrenchment prevented the Report's glaring lack of serious research and breadth of vision being exposed at the time. Such questions, as the worth and usefulness of purpose-built youth centres, the training and recruitment of voluntary part-time workers, the relationship between the Youth Service and other welfare agencies, the funding of the service, male predominance amongst staff and the orientation of provision towards the needs of young males and the appropriate legalistic position of the Youth Service apropos of central and local government,[77] were areas barely, if at all, discussed. Compared with the Russell, Crowther, Robbins, Newsom and Plowden Reports, Albemarle is almost a travesty which has in many ways ill-served an already under-privileged sector of the education service, where both expertise and finance have long been at a premium. Given the newly found commitment of the Government towards youth work in 1960 Albemarle was in many ways a lost opportunity.

3   Thinking it out

The Albemarle Report, as noted in the previous chapter, heralded the advent of a new era in youth work. It injected into an almost moribund service an air of confidence and buoyancy that had been absent for many years. The building programme that coincided with its publication, the money it appeared to release from central government funds for the expansion of LEA provision and the training programmes it engendered for those recruited into full-time youth work, were on the surface solid enough achievements. In reality the influence of the Albemarle Report was probably far more symbolic than real, providing the Government with a public *raison d'être* for policies that were already largely pre-ordained.[1]

LEAs that already possessed established policies relating to Youth Service provision for young people simply tended to accept gratefully the 'Albemarle Money', as it was called, and continued as before. As an HMI's report on West Sussex notes:[2]

> the LEA had looked critically at the quality of its Youth Service to see what contributions it was making to the needs of adolescents . . . . As a result of this review, which was undertaken prior to the Albemarle Report, the LEA decided that a programme of development was needed . . . . It was, therefore, decided to appoint to the staff of each secondary school a Youth Tutor who would have few day-time teaching responsibilities and whose work would consist of the establishment of informal educational activities in the evenings for pupils over 14 years of age and for young people in their first few years of employment. Those who became members of these groups would have the use of the school's premises and equipment and Youth Wings would be built at the schools to provide social centres.

Clearly those authorities such as West Sussex that were already committed, or merely pre-disposed, to creating school-based provision as opposed to free-standing youth centres were in no way deflected from this course of action by Albemarle. Albemarle paid the piper but made scant effort to call the tune. Other LEAs, like Hertfordshire, who envisaged only a very limited role for LEA provision, simply increased the size of their grant-aid to voluntary organizations operating within their area as the funds available to them grew. Overall, the effect of Albemarle was very uneven according to the philosophy and commitment of the various LEAs to youth work.

The Report had clearly highlighted the wide variations in LEA expenditure on the youth sector. For example, at one extreme Essex was spending for each young person in its area aged fifteen to twenty £2 7s 0d per annum in 1957-8, compared to the meagre 1s 6d per annum set aside by Bootle.[3] The financial floodgates opened by Albemarle meant that LEAs with little or no experience of running centres or employing staff on either a full-time or paid part-time basis[4] became obliged to draw up and implement a development plan for an area of activity in which they had previously exhibited scant interest. For many this amounted to little more than searching out a seemingly successful formula operating elsewhere and replicating it within their own area. Such a package was near at hand, for an experimental LEA centre at Withywood, on the outskirts of Bristol, provided the blue-print for a Ministry of Education Building Bulletin[5] that was both widely circulated and praised. This offered many LEAs an easy way out of their dilemma regarding what type of youth provision to develop, and led to a situation where, as an architect explains: 'many replicas seem to have occurred, often built out of context with the Bristol suburban situation. Also short-comings, particularly the cramped entrance and cloaks area, have been repeated with little improvement.'[6]

The open plan Withywood style centre had been designed to offer: 'an uninterrupted space or series of linked spaces, sub-divided by partial or discontinuous screens, within which social, practical, physical and cultural activities can be pursued in harmony.'[7] With its coffee bar, lounge area, workshops, quiet room and sophisticated decor the Withywood style unit was paradoxically best suited for the re-creation of a social discotheque environment; this, contemporary wisdom maintained, would prove especially attractive to the over eighteens. This group, however, were generally those least attracted to the youth centre, for whatever its facilities it still lacked a licensed bar, and in consequence they in the main opted to frequent the pubs and commercial clubs that private enterprise developed to cater for precisely this potentially profitable clientele. The youth centres, so often designed with this age group in mind became all too often for the eighteen plus merely a port of last resort, the clubs becoming in the words of one leader 'merely somewhere to go when they ran out of money'.[8]

A form of Gresham's Law came into play, whereby the absence in any substantial number of those aged eighteen and over meant that inevitably the bulk of membership was drawn from amongst those at the lower end of the statutory age spectrum. As those 'young people at the top end of the age range (fourteen to twenty) find little identity with the people at the bottom end of the age range'.[9] The end result has been a cumulative one whereby an ever more beleaguered minority of older members have been driven to join their peers outside the orbit of the youth centre. Attempts to correct this imbalance by artificially dividing up the age groups through the introduction of separate 'Junior' and 'Senior' nights have done little to alleviate the problem, for chronological age does not always reflect social maturity, and inevitably the arbitrarily chosen dividing line between 'Junior' and 'Senior' membership cuts across peer groups, particularly cross-sexual friendship patterns usually involving younger girls and older boys. On paper the categorization of members by age may appear attractive, but in practice youth leaders often find it difficult to operate particularly in centres not attached to schools where the genuine age of an individual client is in many instances difficult to ascertain. Increasingly youth clubs have found themselves as a result of this age drift stigmatized as the haunt of the younger adolescent, as Ince found in his survey: 'When the young people started to earn their living at 15, they felt too sophisticated for Youth Clubs. They put these "behind" them along with school and other symbols of "childhood".'[10]

Unfortunately the buildings of the type advocated in Building Bulletin No. 20 were not designed to either provide for or contain many of the more vigorous activities that the younger members have come to expect of the club environment. For example, it dismissed the traditional gymnasium as not offering 'the right kind of space for the physical activities of a general mixed club', thus obliging the youth workers either to prohibit the playing of all but the most genteel games or allowing them in the general social area where they intrude upon other activities and create an ever present danger of injury, damage or conflict. The open-plan layout also means that areas cannot be easily isolated or locked up to reduce the area requiring supervision when the numbers attending a club session are low, so at all times a healthy complement of staff is essential simply to control vandalism. The decor of the Withywood type centre is perfectly suited for the needs of adult groups and the older adolescents whom it was envisaged would be major users of the centres for dancing, quiet recreational pursuits and as clients of the coffee-bar, but all too often it has proved simply not robust enough for the more strenuous and active 'games' of the younger members. They now stand in numerous districts, battered, vandalized, seedy and, in many cases, under-used but over-staffed. Certainly the disillusionment felt in many quarters with those units was reflected in the Youth Service Development Council Report, which urged a fresh perspective that would distance the Youth Service 'from the club-is-the-Youth Service approach' and replace it with the challenge implicit in 'meeting the needs of young people by making contact with them wherever they are'.[11]

The YSDC Report was also an honest recognition of the fact that a comprehensive service could not be provided by the clubs alone and that in many areas there already existed too many of the wrong sort in the wrong place. In global terms the building programme that followed Albemarle could not be described as over-ambitious, but compared with previous levels of Youth Service expenditure it was remarkable. A great deal of it was unfortunately spent with little thought as to the needs of either the clientele or the staff. Whereas the Boys' Club Movement had over generations developed a policy regarding the design of buildings that would complement its pattern of provision and style of work,[12] the statutory sector grew in this area too quickly for such a process to take place. Withywood was an exciting and imaginative experiment, sadly, however, in their haste far too many LEAs chose to replicate it before its worth had been evaluated and they have in consequence often paid a high price for their lack of planning and research.

Staffing the Youth Service

The first priority according to the evaluation of needs set out by the Albemarle Committee had been 'the setting in hand of arrangements for both the emergency and long-term training of professional leaders.'[13] This led to the establishment of a National College for the Training of Youth Leaders, which was opened in Leicester[14] in 1961, and offered a one year training course in youth leadership for mature students, supplementing the already existing courses operating at University College, Swansea, Westhill College (Birmingham), Liverpool (the National Association of Boys' Clubs) and London (the National College of the YMCA).

The National College did not however simply augment the established institutions, but acquired from the onset the status of a 'first amongst equals', not least because its student body exceeded that of all the other training agencies combined. By 1970 its former students occupied one-third of all full-time youth posts, with these concentrated in the statutory sector where according to Parr's study they provided 41 per cent of the leaders.[15]

It would not be too much of an exaggeration to call the National College the staff college of the LEA sector, not only because so many of its ex-students now hold senior management positions in that sector,[16] but also because of the unique role it played in establishing the post-Albemarle tenor of the Youth Service. The National College was a new and in many ways unique institution obliged from the onset to innovate whilst simultaneously preparing students for a working environment that was itself undergoing a period of rapid change and growth. By definition it had few institutions which it could either relate to or cross-fertilize with. This absence of any tradition on which to build coupled with the brief time-scale that existed between its inception and the arrival of the first batch of students allowed precious little opportunity for it to formulate its own ethos. Yet despite these formidable handicaps it did succeed, as Ewen notes, in creating a style of youth leadership that was recognizably its own:[17]

> Whilst the College purported to have no particular 'slant', it is clear that the professional ethos that emerged included such attitudes as non-directiveness, non-judgementalism, acceptance and so forth; some of these attitudes, which have resulted in a movement away from 'youth leadership' towards 'youth work' are at variance with much of the motivation which lies behind the volunteer's involvement in youth work. There would appear to be a considerable lack of consensus between the expectations of youth work of the volunteer and those of the professional.

The value and worth of much of the theory to which Ewen refers is still hotly debated but it has none the less helped to formulate a professional style that is unique to the full-time elite of youth workers. Serving at times to 'ward off criticism from outside the fraternity'[18] it has inevitably in doing so distanced the full-time professional from the part-time untrained volunteers who numerically dominate the Youth Service. Often this 'style' is passed on to the part-time youth workers in abbreviated form, as training designed to 'change attitudes' and create a 'fresh approach', in a language that for many must seem strange and mystifying.[19] As Dearling shows in an extreme, but perhaps not all that atypical case, the professional worker may enforce the non-directive, non-judgmental methodology upon his or her part-time assistants with as much rigidity as his more formal activity-based colleagues. For it can be, and often is, structured into a system of 'Recording Forms' that elicit from the part-time worker the type, value and volume of the personal contacts shared with members during a session, until in Dearling's words:[20]

> The form is somehow sacrosanct, and it serves the dual purpose of regulating the type of work engaged in at the club and in particular, providing a 'professionalisation' of the work undertaken by the part-time youth leader, for in recording things on paper, the work of the individual grows in status.

As in adult education, the much vaunted 'informality' of much contemporary youth work is often carefully cocooned within an 'inflexible bureaucratic structure'[21] that reinforces the established orthodoxy through a supervisory network that is often internalized to the extent that its inherent contradictions are concealed even from the participants. As in this example taken from an unattached youth work project report:[22]

> The male worker especially did not have any confidence in the counsellor in her supervisory role, and he became increasingly concerned about what he considered to be her complete lack of direction. He resigned from the project in June in order to take up Child Care work.

One of the problems that emanates from a situation in which the professional 'takes over from and excludes the volunteer is that . . . [it] leaves the volunteer with no other role than that of critic'.[23] The National College and the other centres of full-time training that have opened since 1961, undoubtedly have created a new style of youth work and injected a more professional approach, but in so doing they appear to have widened the gap between the full-timer and the volunteer. The latter is often puzzled and confused not only by the jargon but is also alienated from the style of work it represents. As Eggleston found, the statutory sector is increasingly unwilling to engage, even on an unpaid voluntary basis, workers who are unwilling to undertake training which will integrate him or her into the accepted conceptual norm. Leaders are either recruited direct from training courses or they are:[24]

> usually placed under strong pressure to become 'professional' . . . .
> If he does not, he is likely to find either that his activity is not of continuing relevance to the club or that one of the 'professional' leaders has attended a course that will give him the skills to supplant . . . the leader. If, not withstanding, he remains, he will usually be obliged to stay in a marginal role and be denied the status or title of

'leader'. In short, ways will be found to translate, eliminate or mini-
mise such persons for they represent an unacceptable lay intrusion
into the professional model of the Youth Service.

It was envisaged that the dissonance between full- and part-time
youth leaders would be minimized by the policy of recruiting students
for professional training from amongst mature candidates who had had
experience of youth work in a part-time capacity. Thus it was accepted
practice, even before the McNair and Jackson Reports gave it official
approval, to recruit the cadre of full-time workers from the ranks of
those who had experience of industry or commerce. The mature
student cum entrant was legislated for by the simple device of setting
a minimum age for admission to a training course.[25] An incidental
consequence of this policy has been that the courses have tended to
recruit a socially atypical group of personnel to full-time youth work,
which presumably is quite the reverse of the original intention underlying this criteria for entry. As Hopper and Osborn have shown, mature-
adult students undertaking full-time courses tend, for example, towards
'rejection of the high value which they feel society has placed on money
and status'.[26] They are also likely to be drawn from amongst those for
whom:[27]

> an alternative life-style constitutes a substitute goal, one which they
> adopt after failing to achieve their earlier expectations concerning
> income and status . . . [thus] . . . . By virtue of their history of
> failure in the labour market, many develop a low sense of self-
> esteem coupled with highly ambivalent attitudes towards their own
> abilities.

This 'problem' relating to student recruitment was not initially apparent, for the National College and other training agencies during the
early growth period, immediately following Albemarle, for at that
juncture they concentrated upon the recruitment of students from the
sizeable pool of unqualified full-time youth leaders already in post and
from the considerable number of highly motivated voluntary part-time
workers, who during that period saw an expanding Youth Service emerging that would offer them a challenging and worthwhile career. As
Watkins notes, this meant that with regard to the National College,
'almost without exception students had had experience of youth work
as . . . full-time leaders . . . part-time leaders, assistants or helpers, paid
or unpaid.'[28] As this reservoir of potential students inevitably dimin-
ished, so gradually the intake appears to have been supplemented by

students who tended to conform to the Hopper and Osborn model. This has resulted in a growing number of students who have displayed a marked reluctance, upon completion of their training, to apply for posts involving either youth club or community centre management.

By 1974 when a National Association of Youth Service Officers survey revealed a short-fall of 30.4 per cent in qualified workers for the 2,184 posts then in existence,[29] another study showed that less than 17 per cent of the students graduating from the six major training institutions were entering the Youth Service, statutory or voluntary.[30] In fact the Youth Service was failing to recruit enough newly qualified staff to keep pace with the number of new posts being created, let alone with the wastage and loss of staff who for various reasons were leaving full-time youth work. As Jones concluded, the staffing situation was such that by 1975:[31]

> Whether the Albemarle Committee was right or wrong in placing its main emphasis on the need to provide more buildings and more workers is now immaterial. The fact is that we have more buildings, but not nearly enough staff to man them.

One disturbing side-effect of this acute staff shortage is that it obviates against a realistic probationary period for the newly qualified:[32]

> Beginners in the occupation find that there is no recognised way in which they can develop the skill newly acquired in training, through, for example, assistants posts for a probationary period. Many of them choose and others are forced to undertake jobs on leaving their training agencies which are too big for them. Some are defeated by the job and leave the service.

Others, one may assume, lack the initial confidence to embark upon the jobs that are offered and simply find alternative employment, where possible, in allied fields.

Even the growth in levels of unemployment amongst teachers and community workers in recent years does not appear to have radically altered the situation. The Youth Service still remains unattractive even to those whom it trains, a fact that one would have expected to generate serious discussion and self-questioning amongst both employing agencies and trainers alike. Unfortunately, at the time of writing, no such debate appears to have developed and students continue to vote with their feet.[33]

The Albemarle Committee, like similar bodies before it, recognized that no amount of specialist training units would of themselves be able to produce the requisite number of qualified staff needed to meet the requirements of an expanded Youth Service. They saw as a solution to this difficulty the recruitment into youth work of trained teachers. This prognosis had the added advantage of helping to solve the seemingly intractable problem of how to create a career structure for specialist youth workers. Albemarle accepted that such is the nature of full-time youth work, with its isolation and anti-social hours that it was realistic to accept that 'youth leadership is a life-long career for only a few'.[34] Given this, it would be difficult to attract into the service on a full-time basis mature individuals of the right calibre, for these would be unlikely to leave secure employment, enter college on a grant (with the implied risk of failing to qualify) for the privilege of spending a few years in youth work on a salary that was probably below that they were enjoying in their previous employment. Teachers, on the other hand, could quite painlessly spend a limited number of years in youth work and then return, pension rights, superannuation and incremental points intact, to secondary or further education, where with good fortune their youth experience might conceivably tip the balance in their favour regarding promotion. Indeed, the Albemarle Report promised the teacher who might be interested in devoting a few years to youth work as much, when with precious little justification it predicted: 'we shall expect such experience to rank as a major qualification for posts in county colleges'.[35] These birds of passage, it was assumed, would thus leave the limited number of senior posts in the youth sector available for those individuals whose training left them qualified solely for youth work.

The Albemarle Report talked in terms of between 100 and 120 teachers annually entering the Youth Service.[36] In order to help facilitate this eleven Colleges of Education had by 1963 been encouraged by the Ministry of Education to institute 'youth options' as integrated modules within their Certificate courses. The output from these combined teacher-youth leader courses stood at 124 in 1964, but grew to 593 in 1968, although it is perhaps significant that only one in nine of the students on these courses were aware of their existence before they joined their college.[37] These students, however, did not constitute a net gain for the Youth Service. Clemans in his survey of students on such courses made it clear that:[38]

> although 90% of them will do at least some youth work (full-time or part-time) during their teaching careers . . . most youth tutors in the colleges emphasise that they are training teachers first and foremost. Almost without exception they encourage their students to go into teaching first.

Given the sting in the tail of this quote it is not surprising that this method of staff recruitment through dual training courses has been less successful than was initially expected. Button found that despite the fact that those who entered full-time youth work were in the main financially better off than their colleagues who had gone into teaching only 19 out of 80 men and 2 out of 86 women who had completed a dual course in 1963 were by 1966 in full-time youth work.[39] Considerable numbers of teachers have been enlisted, but not noticeably via this route. Far more effective as a means of attracting trained teachers and graduates into youth work has been the expansion of school-based youth work and teaching. This coupled with the avowed policy of a growing minority of LEAs to employ only trained teachers or graduates for posts that entail close liaison with schools and other educational establishments has both attracted more teachers into youth work and simultaneously curtailed the employment prospects of the two-year trained youth and community worker.

The growing influx of teachers into the youth sector appears not only to have restricted the employment opportunities open to the newly qualified two-year trained worker,[40] but to have also adversely affected the career prospects of those already in post. In this respect Chivers found that of the full-time youth workers interviewed for his survey over 75 per cent 'expected and wanted to continue . . . as youth workers'.[41] However a third of these were qualified teachers who significantly: 'had been drawn to youth work in part at least because of its better career opportunities compared to school teaching.'[42] So, presumably, changes in either the pay or management structure of the schools might conceivably reverse this trend leading to a net out-flow of teachers from the Youth Service. Certainly the depth of the long-term commitment of the teachers interviewed by Chivers is difficult to gauge whatever their protestations, for less than 20 per cent of them 'were even approaching middle-life (forty years or more)',[43] and nearly half of them had only been in post for less than two years. In the light of Parr's earlier research, which showed that 57.7 per cent of the LEA appointees he interviewed had only been in full-time youth work for three years or less,[44] it appears that a high level of mobility is the norm in this sector.

What cannot be in dispute however is the growing re-orientation in the patterns of staffing. Fisher found as early as 1972 that: 'significantly more teacher-trained personnel were entering youth and community work than personnel taking up appointments from the full-time Youth and Community Work Training Courses.'[45] Godby and Key, quoted earlier, show that the reason for this reversal of the recruitment model envisaged by Albemarle is not the result of a failure on the part of the various training agencies to produce their required quota of qualified certificated youth and community workers. It is rather, one may assume, a reflection of a shift in the career aspirations on the part of those students and of the expressed preference amongst certain LEAs for the more 'academically' qualified teacher or graduate.[46] Not surprisingly, given many of the trends that have emerged during the last decade, one commentator has described the two-year training courses in youth and community work as 'a one way ticket to oblivion'.[47] A view endorsed by Haywood:[48]

> Most youth workers find professional mobility extremely difficult to achieve. They are not trained to move into education in schools or colleges, or into social, remedial or care work. They are thus prevented from full partnership with other professional workers, and quite unable to bring their particular and unique skills to bear in related fields or professions, or to move about among them. The career structure is poor and carries a bar, not of efficiency but of recognition.

The logistics of the problem outlined by Haywood and Barnsley are widely known, and reforms have been advocated,[49] but the situation has not altered during the intervening years. In fact in one aspect it may well have deteriorated. The reduction in the level of teacher training during recent years has encouraged many colleges to inaugurate two-year youth and community courses as a means of diversifying staff and preventing redundancies.[50] It is a trend that has been endorsed by the DES and LEAs alike, on the grounds that such courses might help to alleviate the acute staff shortage in the Youth Service. The appearance of these new courses, that are in all respects identical to those previously in existence, can only make the implementation of any reforms more rather than less difficult and further spread even more thinly the limited number of potential students who are of the right calibre and background, and who possess the motivation and experience to both contribute to and benefit from such a course. The growing numbers of two-year trained workers entering the job-market has not led to the creation of an adequate career structure that takes cognizance of their skills, and so they remain, particularly in a period of contracting demand, singularly ill-equipped to compete with certificated teachers, graduate teachers and the growing numbers of graduates with a relevant post-graduate qualification. Is it any wonder then that many of these students choose to avoid the second class and dead-end appointments they are offered in the Youth Service and seek alternative employment. The debates concerning the quality, quantity and training of the professional cadre of youth workers have tended to obscure and divert attention from what in reality should be the Youth Service's major staffing concern, namely the needs of the workers who perform the vast bulk of the face to face work with clients; the unpaid, unqualified and untrained volunteers. It has been estimated by the ex-Director of the National Youth Bureau that the ratio of full-time youth workers to part-time ones stands in the region of 1 to a 1,000[51] yet the Albemarle Report made only one recommendation concerning the training of these voluntary leaders. This was that they should spend one month observing a professional worker carrying out his or her duties prior to taking responsibility for the management of a club or centre of their own.[52] Given the paucity of qualified full-time workers in post and their uneven distribution around the country the total impracticability of this suggestion was quickly realized and two committees were established to examine the question of the feasibility of introducing some form of in-service training for voluntary workers.

Both the Bessey Report,[53] published in 1962, and the Youth Service Development Council (YSDC) document produced in 1966,[54] advocated the setting up of Area Training Committees that would offer a unified training programme to all part-time workers employed in both the statutory and voluntary sectors. Despite considerable initial goodwill on both sides, all but two of the Area Training Committees have ceased to function and the joint approach has proved nothing less than an 'abysmal failure'.[55] The uniformed organizations have since the publication of the Bessey Report maintained and even strengthened their own autonomous training schemes, while the major religious groupings sponsoring youth groups taking their lead from Bessey have begun to operate courses for their own voluntary workers.[56] Except where these voluntary groups are in receipt of LEA grant-aid to cover the salary of their part-time worker, they have displayed a marked reluctance to sacrifice the independence that accrues from the maintenance of a separate training course. The Bessey Courses, (as the basic training courses are often called) are organized under the tutelage of an LEA appointed Training Officer[57] and have largely become the reserve of paid and voluntary staff working in LEA sponsored or grant-aided units. The LEA courses have inevitably tended to reflect the needs and ethos of their paymaster, and excellent though many of them are they are only managing to meet a fraction of the overall demand.

The failure of the Area Training Committees to develop a unified training programme for the Youth Service has been due in part to a belief amongst certain voluntary organizations that such courses are an attempt to produce increased uniformity of provision. It was a belief that could hardly have been allayed by the oft quoted remark of one LEA organizer that his aim was 'to wipe the inefficient voluntary organizations off the map',[58] or by the way in which many of the courses were set up and managed. The report on the Teesside Joint Training Agency illustrates the extent to which LEAs came to dominate the post-Bessey structures:[59]

> Arising out of a resolution of the Chief Education Officer's Committee of the North East Council of Education Committees, a meeting of chief officers and their Youth Officers was held in Middlesbrough. The Authorities of Darlington, Durham, Middlesbrough, West Hartlepool and the North Riding of Yorkshire were represented. They met to consider arrangements for the establishment of training courses for part-time youth leaders in the area . . . . The meeting recommended the establishment of a Co-ordinating Committee to represent the Authorities of the area and to ensure comparable standards between courses . . . . In order to ensure consultation with the voluntary organisations, representatives of the Standing Conference of Voluntary Youth Organizations for Durham and the North Riding were invited . . . Teesside now run several courses . . . tutoring has been in almost all cases, carried out by Youth Officers in each Authority.

Unfortunately the longer the voluntary organizations remain on the periphery of the common training programme, for whatever reasons, then the greater the temptation amongst LEAs to adopt the courses and their curriculum to suit their own specialized needs.[60] Certainly evidence already exists that a number of LEAs take little cognizance of the needs of voluntary organizations when planning their courses and use them as a means of recruiting staff for their own clubs and centres.[61] The failure of the voluntary and statutory sectors to work effectively in unison at this level has shown the extent to which much of the talk concerning 'partnership' has been little more than 'lip-service',[62] and just how premature Barnes was in 1948 when he predicted that 'the old distinction between official and voluntary agencies is breaking down as far as youth work is concerned'.[63]

New approaches

The Albemarle Report devoted a great deal of space to justifying the expansion of the Youth Service, to the need for more trained full-time staff and to administrative questions such as finance, but it showed a certain reluctance to evaluate and choose between conflicting approaches to youth work and the future direction the expanded service it favoured should take. Its bland acceptance of a social control function for the service, coupled with its apparent ability to reverse the steady erosion and decline in levels of provision that had taken place during the preceding decade not surprisingly ensured it, as already noted, an overwhelmingly enthusiastic reception amongst interested parties. In the words of one writer it was and often still is treated 'with awe'.[64]

The Albemarle Report was a consensus document that aroused little if any controversy following its publication, primarily because it did not recommend further contraction, as many had feared it might, and also because it made no attempt to offer 'advice' to either the voluntary or statutory agencies regarding their methodology. In effect all were to be encouraged to continue operating as they deemed fit, but at a greater intensity.

Simply because Albemarle chose to ignore their presence in no way signifies that profound differences regarding the future role and structure of the Youth Service were non-existent in the late 1950s. They certainly existed and largely related to such issues as the relative merits of club as opposed to school-based provision; the span of the statutory age range; the precise relationship and balance between the voluntary and statutory sectors and to an extent around the question of whether an LEA presence was even beneficial at all.[65] Perhaps the self-confidence gained during the seven years of unparalleled and uninterrupted growth following Albemarle provided the spur, or possibly it was simply that the debates around these issues for so long held in abeyance could no longer be avoided, whatever the motivation the YSDC announced in 1967 the formation of two important study groups. One was to examine the future relationship between the Youth Service and the schools, and was chaired by Andrew Fairbairn, then Deputy Director of Education for Leicestershire; the second was given the task of looking at the community aspects of youth work and the Youth Service potential as an agent for community development; this group was chaired by Fred Milson, then Head of Youth Work at Westhill College of Education.

Upon their completion the two reports were amalgamated and published under the joint title of 'Youth and Community Work in the 70s'.[66]

The Report faced up with refreshing candour to a wide range of issues. For example, it recognized the growing preponderance amongst the clientele of both youth clubs and youth groups of young persons drawn from the lower end and even below the existing statutory age band, and forcefully advocated changes in policy designed to meet the needs of the younger age group. The Report also attempted to enunciate a philosophy for the Youth Service, one that went well beyond that implied but never clearly spelt out in the Albemarle Report, and which offered an alternative to that agreed upon at the 1951 Ashridge Conference. For Fairbairn and Milson the principle role of the Youth Service was to offer young people an educational experience that would better equip them to play an active role as members of a participating democracy. They were to be seen as partners in a society in which they would have both the opportunity and right to be involved in the decision-making process. The Youth Service was to be an agency capable of bestowing upon adolescents the opportunity of 'contracting in' to this decision-making process. If the document had a key-note it was client participation, summed up in the following phrase: 'young people would be encouraged to play an active part in a society which they themselves will help to mould.'[67]

'Youth and Community Work in the 70s' shared many of the attitudes and orientations of the Calouste Gulbenkian study group that prepared the report 'Community Work and Social Change'. The latter report published a year before the Fairbairn-Milson Report even predicted the outcome of the YSDC Report with remarkable accuracy:[68]

> They are likely to conclude that the youth leader of the future will need a much stronger community orientation both in his training and practice. He may well work more closely with other workers and agencies in the community and possibly have responsibilities which are not confined to work with young people.

Inevitably along with this new approach to youth work came a belief that political education had a pivotal role to play in a restructured Youth Service, and as a consequence Fairbairn-Milson raised for the first time in an official document the possibility that the political youth movements should become full partners.[69]

'Youth and Community Work in the 70s' exhibited more than a passing affinity with the ideas of Morrell and the other moving spirits behind the CDP initiative. It did not however produce the same tangible results in terms of governmental investment. One immediate discernible result was, however, the almost over-night redesignation of the existing youth work training courses. All added the appellation community to their prospectus, a response that significantly elicited from the DES a ruling that whatever their title they should continue to restrict themselves 'to the training of youth workers and community centre wardens'.[70] In similar vein it became fashionable for LEA Youth Officers to add the label 'community' to their title; all too often however this change in their designation was more symbolic than real, involving no fundamental reconstruction of their role and duties that might have given the new title some substance.

A number of sympathetic LEAs and organizations such as the Young Volunteer Force Foundation[71] did attempt to put into practice the ideas contained within the Fairbairn-Milson Report, with the result that the fragmentation of the Youth Service acquired an added dimension. Both a number of LEAs and certain leading voluntary organizations rejected the main recommendations of the Report outright[72] with many of the later groups seeing the Report as further evidence of a growing distance between their concept of youth work and what they intuitively sensed to be the new 'official' ideology. The NABC were particularly vehement in their opposition. Dawes describes the YSDC, quite unfairly given the origins of its constituent members, as 'one of those all-knowing, all-seeing Whitehall organisations', and goes on to claim that the Report it sponsored 'pooh-poohed the work of volunteers, decried the traditional idea that youth leaders should attempt to give any kind of lead to the young and argued that in any case clubs were no longer valid'.[73] Indeed to oppose the Report, he continues, would strike a blow against 'the so-called permissive society' and 'trendy sociologists'.

The Fairbairn-Milson Report had been prepared for a Labour Minister of Education, however, following the General Election of June 1970, the decision concerning its implementation resided with the new Conservative Minister. After an eight month delay she announced that: 'The Government do not think it would be right to change the nature of the Service in England and Wales radically by setting up a Youth and Community Service with not very clearly defined responsibilities.'[74]

Given the substantial delay between initial publication of the Report and any official response, and the influential lobbying carried out by certain of the major voluntary bodies opposed to implementation, its rejection, described by Dawes as 'a victory for the voluntary youth movement, and in particular for the boys' clubs',[75] came as a surprise to no one. Shortly before the official pronouncement, Milson in an article published in the *Times Educational Supplement* clearly showed his awareness that the Report was not going to be implemented, and expressed his frustration with the innate conservatism of much contemporary youth work in forceful tones that asked of the Report's opponents:[76]

> Is it right about the primary goal? If not, what would the critics put in its place? That is the question they must answer unless they want youth work to become more and more like the pale second-rate imitation of commercial entertainment for young people, over-dependent on dancing, darts and table-tennis, appealing more and more to the younger male teenager and more and more to the bourgeois and immature.

It is impossible to gauge the extent to which the hostility aroused by 'Youth and Community Work in the 70s' contributed to the demise of the YSDC. However, it was one month after the Minister's rejection of that document, and a full twelve months on from the Committee's last meeting that the DES announced its closure in a statement that went on to reaffirm the Government's intention to retain the existing statutory age band for the Youth Service and to call for: 'closer liaison between voluntary bodies and local authorities, further joint use of premises and whenever possible, the conversion of existing buildings.'[77]

What emerged from the wreckage left in the wake of the Fairbairn-Milson Report was a compromise formula which although reaffirming the centrality of the concept of 'partnership' to the Government's youth policy offered no positive guidelines as to how this might be achieved at either national or local level. The truth of the matter was that, whatever its reasons, the Government was not willing at that juncture to adopt a positive and interventionist youth policy of the kind that would be required to reorientate the Youth Service to meet the needs of the older adolescent. Even though as Dennis Howell, who had served on both the Albemarle Committee and the YSDC, pointed out: 'all the figures presented to us show that there was a fantastic drop-off in the numbers of young people over sixteen associated with the Youth Service.'[78] The result of this policy vacuum was that the voluntary sector largely felt encouraged to continue 'business as usual'. Amongst LEAs, however, many taking their cue from Fairbairn-Milson and the vague pronouncement of the Minister regarding joint use of premises opted to join the drift towards school-based provision, while others, apart from changing the appellation of the responsible officer, adopted a 'wait and see' strategy, for local government reorganization was on the horizon and they saw in the light of this little point in adopting a radically new pattern of provision. This meant that wide variations in

the type and quality of service provided in the various localities continued, not only as a direct consequence of a lack of direction from the
DES, but also due to a reluctance on the part of certain LEAs to invest
scarce resources in informal education. As the following quotation
clearly illustrates, considerable opposition to such provision existed
amongst local government representatives and the balance of forces on
a particular Council inevitably came to be reflected in the levels of
expenditure:[79]

> Cllr. Mrs. M. Wilson: 'I wonder if there's any proof youth clubs
> really do serve a useful purpose?' Cllr. W.B. Secombe pointed out
> that: '18 year olds were now legally adults. They ought not now to
> be treated like little children.' He said of youth clubs 'As for the
> good they do – I'm not impressed!'

Whatever the cause or causes, considerable discrepancies can be discerned in the level of youth provision between different LEAs.[80] They
were not by 1970 as extreme as those highlighted in Appendix Four of
the Albemarle Report, or as those which existed in the levels of nursery
provision in different authorities at this time, but they were wide
enough to merit, one would have thought, an expression of concern
from the DES.

In February 1975, the Under-Secretary of State for Education, Hugh
Jenkins, announced his intention of 'entering into consultation with the
statutory and voluntary youth service interests, and with representatives
of young people about the present and future needs of young citizens
and the role of the Youth Service in a changing society.'[81] This announcement was followed by the circulation of a discussion document
issued by the DES in November 1975[82] that was as Ewen notes 'largely a
statement of fact . . . and . . . a statement of support'[83] for the Youth
Service as it existed. It was couched in the most general phraseology
and significantly it avoided making any reference whatsoever to the
growing divide between the conceptual approaches to youth work of
many elements within and between the voluntary and statutory sectors,
to the expanding school-based provision or to the unabated decline in
the numbers of young people over the school-leaving age who maintained
any affiliation, however slight, with any youth organization. Further-
more, it gave no indication as to either future government policy or
possible levels of expenditure on the youth sector.

Regarding the Discussion Paper's open-ended call for 'a reappraisal
of provision and identification of appropriate roles, objectives and
clients',[84] it can only be said that it appears to have generated little

productive debate, apart from, that is, the consultative document published by the National Youth Bureau[85] which was a collection of forty contributions submitted by various organizations, local authorities and individuals on the question of the training and recruitment of full-time youth and community workers. The British Youth Council, the Community and Youth Service Association, the Staff Panel of the Joint Negotiating Committee for Youth Leaders and Community Centre Wardens, the National Association of Youth and Community Education Officers (formerly NAYSO), the National Council of Voluntary Youth Services, and the Youth and Community Work Trainers Association, all submitted brief memorandums to the DES[86] in which each welcomed the document and called for more research, a relaxing of the statutory age limits, the setting up of a permanent consultative body and all dealt at disproportionate length with the question of staff training.

Once again the immediate concerns of the professionals regarding their own status appeared to have tended to push aside other more contentious issues. At least in debating their own professional situation and development the full-time workers could achieve some, albeit limited, measure of unanimity. This unity would have undoubtedly been shattered if the discussions had been broadened out, so all parties appear to have been content to leave well alone, recognizing as one outside body noted 'that no consensus on what should happen to the Youth Service in . . . the next few years is possible'.[87] This accepted, the major parties opted for a retreat into the not very distant past and a safe acceptance of the lowest possible common denominator as the price of consensus by calling for the setting up of a National Consultative Body to advise the DES on matters relating to Youth Service policy. It amounted to little more than a request for the resurrection of the YSDC which had operated between 1960 and 1971 and whose final report had created such a furore. There the general will evaporated, as no agreement amongst the various parties could be found as to its component parts, size or powers, thus leaving the DES to once more 'play the unwanted role of referee in a game with no rules'.[88]

4 An uneasy marriage: schools and the Youth Service

The DES Discussion Document in failing to mention, let alone discuss and evaluate, the impact of school-based youth work succeeded in avoiding 'what is probably the most critical and complex issue in the Youth Service'.[1] This was not, however, an unusual omission, for as Hamilton had noted three years earlier:[2]

> Youth workers seem to be burying their heads in the sand. And allowing themselves, with no debate, to be quietly moved into more formal situations. It is in these situations such as the school, where any hope that they had of working for the young and reversing this process is nearly impossible.

In fact, the transfer of resources into school-based youth work had, according to Booton, by 1975 reached the stage where 'almost 50 per cent of all statutory provision is now irrevocably tied to the system of secondary education'.[3] A transfer that meant that this type of provision was consuming 'between 35 per cent and 40 per cent of all statutory staff'.[4]

In part this shift in emphasis can be seen as an attempt on the part of some LEAs to comply with the recommendations of the Newsom Report that urged them to ensure that 'the ultimate responsibility for the pupils welfare up to the age of 16 should rest with the schools and the education programme, though increasingly outward looking should be school-based'.[5] Given this conceptual model, Newsom later in the Report, somewhat reluctantly one feels, felt obliged to suggest:[6]

> that if the school day is extended, some element of compulsion will have to be introduced into what are now voluntary activities. Otherwise, it will be impossible to plan the programme as a coherent whole, or to estimate the total needs in terms of staffing and facilities, and hence to justify additional expenditure .... It would undoubtedly be a pity if school clubs had to lose their essentially voluntary nature, but this would be partly offset by the fact that many schools would be able to offer a much wider range of regular activities than they now find possible; and a large element of personal

choice could be preserved for pupils within the general requirement
to take part in this side of the school life. There is too, to be considered the fact that some of the pupils who live in the most adverse
environments and who most need to be guided into healthy recreational pursuits, will not take part if these are on an entirely optional
basis.

Even when one makes full allowance for the good intentions that inspired this suggestion it still remains a somewhat disturbing statement
of intent coming as it does from an influential and semi-official group
of educationalists and lay people. Bertrand Russell once wrote that 'no
political theory is adequate unless it is applicable to children as well as
men and women'.[7] Sixty years on this still seems a sound guide-line for
the evaluation of an educational innovation. It is certainly one that
when applied to the changes suggested by Newsom exposes both its
dangerous paternalism and the failure of the Committee to grasp the
motivation and principles that are the corner-stone not only of youth
work but of all informal, non-vocational education. If youth work is
envisaged as an exercise in participatory democracy as Milson and
Fairbairn suggested, then it can hardly be expected to effectively co-
exist with the element of compulsion implicit in the Newsom scenario.
This has a great deal in common with the compulsory hobbies, games
and cadet corps membership that is enforced in certain public schools,
but little with the voluntary concept that has always been a fundamental premise of the Youth Service. To quote Russell once more, the
task of liberal education, as he saw it, is:[8]

> to give a sense of the value of things other than domination, to help
> to create wise citizens of a free community, and through the com-
> bination of citizenship with liberty in individual creativeness to
> enable men to give to human life that splendour some few have
> shown that it can achieve.

The compulsory, manipulated leisure advocated by Newsom obviously
runs counter to this vision and could conceivably prove, if introduced,
to be counter-productive as a means of inculcating the leisure patterns
it is endeavouring to engender, and like the earlier war-time experiment
in directed leisure for young persons could well create managerial and
administrative problems that undermine its effectiveness from the onset.

For many LEAs struggling to increase youth and community provision on a restricted budget, Newsom, along with other policy statements,
particularly that of Mrs Thatcher (2 April 1971) and Fairbairn-Milson,

can only have encouraged them to examine more closely the feasibility of developing the dual and multiple use of school premises. Given other substantial changes taking place within the secondary sector during the 1960s and 1970s, the integration of youth provision within a school setting must often have appeared to be a logical and complementary extension of the developing pastoral and counselling services of the schools. The growth of formalized pastoral care in its many guises led to the appearance of a new, or at least an alternative, definition in educational parlance of a 'good' school. No longer, for many education-alists, was academic achievement to be the sole criterion for measuring success. It was obliged henceforth to compete with another evaluation based upon the degree to which it, as a school, offered a complete educational environment for its pupils.[9] The percentage of pupils persuaded to remain at a school voluntarily beyond the statutory leaving age became an accepted counter-balance to the league table of exam successes that often served as an indicator of a school's proficiency, and LEAs through their capitation system reward the 'successful' school and its staff accordingly.[10]

'Staying-on' for many pupils thus became an end in itself, particularly for those who could expect to pass few, if any, external examinations. The schools themselves often, prior that is to the 'Raising of the School Leaving Age' (ROSLA), brought considerable moral pressure, if not actual blackmail, to bear upon all but their most egregious pupils in the form of veiled threats relating to the possible quality of their leaving reports and employment potential, in order to cajole pupils into com-pleting an additional year. Such was the cumulative effect of this policy of 'persuasion' that ROSLA when it finally reached the Statute Book was in many areas little more than an administrative recognition of a changed reality.[11] The numbers involved in ROSLA for all but a limited number of schools and authorities were usually small enough to ensure the minimal dislocation of existing practice, a fact aided by the intro-duction and spread of the CSE, particularly Mode 3, and the subsequent restructuring of GCE 'O' levels which helped to ensure that a measure of academic success was within the grasp of virtually all scholars.[12] As a result the so-called ROSLA debate all too often was reduced to an embarrassing charade, concerned less with the formulation of a mean-ingful curriculum relevant to the older secondary pupil and more with the discipline problems that it was expected would be posed by the handful of reluctant pupils forced by ROSLA to remain at school for an extra year against their will. The value and the content of the addi-tional year was by and large taken as given and self-evident, with the

inevitable result that probably the most far reaching changes wrought
by ROSLA have been in the rapid growth of pastoral structures within
the secondary school, structures designed to adapt the older pupils to
the school and so enable the schools to avoid the radical changes that
would be entailed in adjusting their practice to meet the needs of the
older pupil, reluctant or not.

The raising of the statutory leaving age to sixteen had the immediate
effect of reducing the level of unemployment amongst adolescents,
however once the initial effect of the drop in the number of leavers in
1973 had been negated by the rise in the numbers leaving in 1974 the
long-term trend, which had been discernible since 1961, of a growing
incidence of unemployed amongst this age group continued unabated.[13]
It is also extremely doubtful that ROSLA has influenced the patterns
and distribution of adolescent unemployment. Certainly American
research indicates that the mere extension of the period of compulsory
schooling in no way improves the competitiveness in the job market of
those young people who, for whatever reason, find themselves least able
to secure employment, for as Collins notes: 'The quality of schools
themselves, and the nature of dominant student cultures suggest that
schooling is very inefficient as a means of training work skills.'[14]
Basically the end-product of the raising of the school-leaving age is that
the same young people end up on the dole queue, they are merely better
academically qualified when they do so.[15] As Parkin notes, any equal-
ization in educational attainment where and when it occurs tends to
produce a re-definition of the attributes that are held to be essential for
success at a given job; for example this may be achieved simply:[16]

> by making the assessment of 'character' an important part of the
> selection process. Because the kinds of personal attributes that go to
> make up character are not generally open to objective measurement,
> the assessment of such attributes can be made by the occupants of
> privileged positions. To insist on character qualifications and not
> merely evidence of 'mere' ability is a method of controlling access to
> positions. This is because the kinds of qualities defined as 'good' are
> more likely than not to be those possessed by members of the dom-
> inant class, and the product of a certain kind of social training.

The evidence indicates that only a marginal amount of upward social
mobility is achieved through education, or for that matter by any other
channel.[17] Certainly no evidence has been forthcoming to indicate that
ROSLA has achieved any positive results in this direction. Indeed it
may well have been counter-productive, for by concentrating resources

during the late 1960s and 1970s on ROSLA provision[18] the Government gave the often erroneous impression that 'at last something positive was being done for the early leaver and the academically less able', and in doing so consumed scarce resources and diverted attention away from the inadequate provision being made through part-time further education for the sixteen to nineteen year olds, and in particular the girls in that age band.[19]

In opposition the Labour Party had stressed that: 'our first priority will be to accommodate those who have no further contact with the education service after leaving school.'[20] The sawdust promises of opposition parties are of course an integral part of electioneering, but it is none the less a pity that this particular policy objective has shown little sign of being implemented. For expenditure in this area has often proved far more effective as a means of generating the acquisition of the scarce occupational skills, that are required by the under-privileged if they are to compete in a highly competitive labour market, than the 'General Studies', 'ROSLA' and Mode Three CSE courses that schools offer and which often amount to little more than a second-rate exposure to academic subjects of questionable relevance and doubtful veracity.[21] For, as Wilby confirms: 'Below grade one (which is equivalent, in any case, to an 'O' level) the possession of a C.S.E. confers no advantage in earnings over those with no school-leaving qualifications at all.'[22]

For many educationalists, ROSLA was an act of faith. A tangible expression of their belief that schools and schooling are beneficial for all young people and as such are an undoubted force for good in society.[23] As one Director of Education stressed, such is the intrinsic value of schooling that:[24]

> it is undesirable for school children to have to cast off from school control suddenly; it should be a gradual process spread over the last two years of compulsory schooling. The Youth Service is a most appropriate agency to aid this process.

The views expressed in the last sentence encapsulate what many feel to be the primary role of the Youth Service in the future. The expansion of full-time schooling so that it now embraces all the young people who fall within the age bracket from which the bulk of the Youth Service's clientele are drawn, could not fail to inspire a self-generating logic that, if accepted, will lead to an increasing subordination of the Youth Service to the needs of the schools. Both bureaucratically and economically separate provision would become markedly difficult to justify without resorting to an intellectual stance akin to that of Illich, Reimer and other de-schoolers. A position that might well be tenable for certain voluntary or community-based youth workers but it is hardly a stance that would be feasible for an LEA Youth Officer to adopt, who is after all a relatively junior official operating within an Education Department dominated by those whose prime responsibility is managing schools and allied services.

Not only ROSLA, but also the growth in the number of LEAs adopting a comprehensive system, helped to fuel the impetus towards the amalgamation of the statutory sector with the schools. For, as one commentator stresses, comprehensivization both created and gave greater rein to those:[25]

> heads and teachers ambitious to extend their own areas of responsibility. The concept of 'school' as the centre of the local community, with its facilities and staff acting as a social service for all ages has found powerful advocates in those committed to the Comprehensive School and the idea of the overwhelming advantages of very large units.

This manifestation of educational imperialism disguised as rationalization has led increasingly to both the Youth Service and non-vocational adult education being subsumed within the school system, often under the guise of creating a network of community schools or colleges. It has been a policy that has not been confined to the United Kingdom for as Simpson found throughout Western Europe, 'the movement for separate accommodation has lost impetus'.[26] Both Phelan and Simpson arrived at the same conclusion, namely that the policy of creating large multiple-use units has emanated to a great extent from 'attitudes towards capital investment which permeate Government and Local Government thinking',[27] rather than from purely educational motives, as the following Scottish Education Department Circulars indicate:[28]

> Education Authorities should bear in mind that the need for community centre and youth club buildings may sometimes be most economically met either by an addition to an existing school or other educational establishment or by the erection of a building sufficiently near such premises to enable advantage to be taken of common services or other facilities.

In the later one it was suggested that:[29]

> Education Authorities might wish to consider, for example, the advantages of providing youth service facilities in buildings designed

to serve other purposes as well, e.g. as part of a school or community centre, and to apply to have the cost of the part allotted to youth activities counted against the investment allocation for the Youth Service. There will be no objection to youth service facilities being used for other purposes, for example, in the afternoons by women's or old people's organizations, when they cannot be used for their main purpose.

This financial compromise has often, to add to the confusion, been dressed up with a great deal of rhetoric that merely serves to disguise the fact that in far too many localities the community school which emerges: 'is merely a new name for play centres, youth clubs and evening centres, with lip-service to Henry Morris, meeting on school premises.'[30]

Given the economic rather than education motivation that lay behind many community schools it is hardly surprising that few accord with the natural boundaries of local communities, or have involved community groups in their planning and development. In the main they have been grafted on to work-a-day schools and obliged, as a result, to create demand and search out need, as in the following example: 'When the Community Activities Organiser of Lawrence Weston School, Bristol, took up his appointment, six thousand questionnaires were sent out asking people on the estate what needs they thought the school might provide for. Only three replies were received.'[31]

For non-vocational adult education the expansion of school-based provision has meant that the style and content of the programme has been increasingly tailored to match the facilities offered by the school and to approximate to the expertise of the staff who are taken as a given resource. Thus adult education can easily become 'subordinated to the school',[32] leading to success being equated with 'the sheer, undifferentiated size of the enrolment'.[33] As Clyne found in his study, venue and accommodation are not incidentals but are a major influence upon both the volume of take-up and the social background of those individuals who choose to involve themselves in adult education:[34]

Special handicaps will often require special facilities and many disadvantaged adults will find informal adult education more acceptable in private houses, clubs, pubs, places of work, clinics or churches. If some 40 per cent of adults have indicated that they have an aversion to education as such it becomes nonsensical to place classes for illiterate adults in traditional school classrooms . . . .
Adult education's important role as a compensatory service will be

strengthened if classes and activities can be divorced from the more traditional and reactionary aspects of school education.

So although non-vocational adult education has gained measurably in terms of plant and expertise from its closer involvement with schools and the community school movement it has been at a price. Certainly expectations that the community school or college would be 'capable of acting as a cultural and recreational focal point'[35] for its designated catchment area has proved wildly optimistic. Undeniably they have a valuable, if limited role to play, but it is essential that these limitations are recognized, for a truly comprehensive adult education service requires that school-based provision is supplemented by alternative and independent facilities that in the words of the 1919 Report allow for 'the fullest self-determination on the part of the students as regards the studies to be pursued, the choice of the teacher and the organisation of the class.'[36]

Regarding young people the problem for the community schools is not one of attracting them on to the campus, it is rather one of retaining their affiliation, for except in areas where selection remains, all the adolescents in a given locality, apart that is from those who leave it to attend denominational or private schools, will have been or are pupils at the school. Obviously factors such as the availability of public transport and the quality and quantity of alternative youth provision will influence the level of take-up, but also of significance, although impossible to quantify, will be the attitude of the adolescents to the school and their relationships with the staff.

It was envisaged by many commentators that a closer liaison between youth work and formal education would acquaint teachers with many of the techniques and skills possessed by youth workers, and which enabled the latter to work successfully with groups of young people who often create acute behaviourial problems within the school environment. As Hogan urged, schools seeking to interest and stimulate these pupils might do worse than appraise the skills and methodology of the successful youth leader:[37]

> who has characteristically accepted as his terms of reference that
> the activity that stirred no response had either to be substantially
> adapted or abandoned . . . very gifted people have demonstrated the
> possibility of achieving a high degree of responsibility, co-operation
> and attainment without dependence on authoritarianism. I wish to
> maintain the simple proposition that schools seeking to enlist the
> loyalty of the adolescent would be extremely unwise to ignore the

techniques developed by those whose work has been carried out in the context of voluntary association. It would be foolish to underestimate the difficulties. Not all teachers and certainly not all heads of schools will find it easy to adapt their attitudes or to provide conditions suitable for adolescents without prejudice to what may be appropriate for somewhat younger children.

If the techniques of control and instruction developed by the Youth Service 'at its best' could help to provide in part an answer to the problem of retaining teacher control within a relatively unstructured school environment, then it was argued might not community development skills give the schools a means of gaining a measure of control over its total environment.[38]

Many schools had long maintained a community face, and on occasions adopted the terminology of community practice,[39] but in the hands of the educational establishment it was transmuted into a fundamentally conservative technique of social intervention. For many teachers community work became an instructional aid capable of being conjured up according to the exigency of the time-table, for the express purpose of procuring from the participating pupils a series of predetermined responses such as 'responsibility, self-confidence and maturity'.[40] As one survey put it: 'Teachers imposed their own values upon youngsters and satisfied their own social consciences vicariously through the efforts of the kids.'[41] In this context community intervention was stripped of its wider social connotations and retained political significance only in so far as: 'all educational practices are profoundly political in the sense that they are designed to produce one sort of human being rather than another.'[42] Where the intention of the school is to nurture in its pupils such traits as 'compassion', 'sympathy' and 'understanding', the chosen personae are selected from social groupings such as the aged, the handicapped and the socially deprived, and these take on the mantle of laboratory specimens, a visual aid whose presence is summoned up and then discarded when the teacher or school assess that the pupils have internalized the 'correct' socially acceptable attitude towards 'them'. To make matters worse, as Griffith found in her survey of such schemes: 'many community service schemes in schools are badly conceived, badly organised and would be better not done at all.'[43]

Such instructional techniques have of course long been commonplace in youth work and have been formalized in such schemes as the Duke of Edinburgh Award and the Community Service Badges awarded by certain uniformed organizations; they are however for all their good intentions profoundly reactionary, for the social position of the 'recipi-ent' is usually taken as fixed and the political implications of need are rarely discussed, so the young person sees need as the end product of a lack of volunteers, or worse the result of individual inadequacies, rather than, as is often the case, as the end product of a mal-distribution of resources. It is therefore the meeting of unequals and can often be humiliating for both parties engaged in the face to face interaction. The community school, however, endeavours to rationalize this established community practice into a far more all-embracing concept by bringing the community into the environs of the school, as well as taking the school into the community.

Attempts to reduce the dissonance between the home and the school, and its environment, have led to the introduction of numerous schemes for the 'packaging' of the pre-school child prior to its admission; play groups, home-visiting and parent support projects have all been initiated in order that the possibility of any clash occurring between the cultures of the home and the school might be minimised. Similarly, it was hoped that the development of the community school or college might help to bridge or eradicate this culture gap where it existed in the secondary sector. As Mays put it, 'the creation of the school as the natural centre of its local community would answer many of our problems',[44] not least, according to Aitken, that of the 'culture clash between home and school'.[45]

If the community school was to become the 'natural centre of its local community' that many of its advocates hoped, then it was only logical that youth, non-vocational adult education, community develop-ment and even to an extent social welfare provision should become its province. It was not however automatically assumed that the acquisition of these functions would radically alter the internal structure of the school. For Midwinter, the community school, within the limitations he acknowledged, was to be a radical departure, an agent for change, not only upon the environment in which it existed, but also upon itself, until 'to be in school is to be in the community; to be in the community is to be in school'.[46]

This vision did not, however, inspire all the proponents of community education, for them, beneath all the fine words and jargon, it was en-visaged as a fundamentally conservative notion, one whereby adjust-ments might be made to the community in order to minimize change within the school. The aim was simply to change just as much as is necessary for everything to go on as before. The co-operation of the home was to be actively sought not in an effort to make the education offered by the school more relevant, but in order to make the price of non-compliance on the part of the pupil higher, the emnity of the school entailing the risk of parental disapproval. The youth club likewise was to be integrated within the school so as to enable the school to exercise a great measure of control over the leisure activities of its pupils,[47] and to give staff the opportunity to reinforce school discipline through the development of informal relationships, for as Phelan noted in his study: 'Those staff who have taken part in the evening programme (youth club activities) have found that their relations with the pupils have improved as a result of the more informal contacts.'[48]

In addition, non-vocational adult education is to be contained within a school setting to eliminate the possibility that it might develop an alternative non-school approach to education, thus in the process appropriating to the school 'the money, men and goodwill available for education and in addition discourage other institutions from assuming educational roles,'[49] – until the school is acknowledged as the sole agent specializing in education, for all but the school selected elites who proceed to further and higher education.

The early expectations that somehow community schools and colleges might establish themselves as 'the focal point of the community' have not been realized, not least because they have, even in rural areas, tended to be based on large units. This has ensured that, almost without exception, the community schools in both rural and urban settings, have been built or developed within no definable community as such. Indeed, often as a matter of policy, to ensure an acceptable mix in the social backgrounds of the pupils, black and white, rich and poor, they have been sited and catchment areas delineated, to enable the schools to draw at minimal cost from as many communities as possible, often only taking a percentage from each. As one Principal has written of his own community school: 'How can there be in Desford a Community College for what is in terms of geography a non-community.'[50]

It is not simply that community schools tend to be badly sited for community use. Equally constricting have been the pre-requisite structural, architectural demands of the day-school, which ensure that the buildings they occupy are at best a compromise between the needs of conflicting client groups, or at worst are uncompromisingly schools that physically make no allowance for other users. As one architect who has been involved in a number of such projects admits:[51]

When considering the educational complex from the point of view of local clubs and societies, one just cannot get away from the fact that basically they are for school children first and secondly for the community. People will not be conned into believing otherwise until . . . the whole complex is open to the community during the daytime. Evening use alone is not enough for the wide range of local organisations and groups.

Access alone is of course only part of the problem, and in itself may often be only symbolic. The core of the problem lies in the extent to which the dead weight of the school imposes itself upon the users long after the pupils and the bulk of the staff have vacated the premises. Overpoweringly the buildings retain the appearance and aura of a school. As Stewart notes, this is pre-eminently the result of economic considerations: 'If we were really to design and open up schools for community use it would dramatically increase costs.'[52] Inevitably the resultant compromise tends to leave all parties to varying degrees dissatisfied with the working environment they inherit. Adult education is squeezed into unsuitable accommodation, in an atmosphere that thrusts its students back into the roles they experienced as schoolpupils. Classroom, decor and furniture all combine to constrict both tutors and students alike, imposing the formalized teaching and learning techniques that Freire dubs 'the Bank system of learning'.[53] This can lead to a total rejection of adult education by those who during their adolescence left school with relief rather than sadness and whose school experience was one of failure rather than one of success: 'Adult education is a middle-class service . . . . Behind it lies the relative success of the middle-class pupil in school – a competitive success or personal pleasure in learning may leave him educationally addicted throughout life.'[54] The research of Hutchinson certainly tends to confirm this.[55] He found that where adult education is contained within a community school campus it attracts an even higher proportion of students from amongst those who have completed a course of higher education and/or are in occupations that place them in social classes II or III than is the norm in free-standing adult education units. Rather than taking nonvocational adult education into the community the community schools seem to have increased attendance by making it even more socially exclusive.

The difficulties created for non-vocational adult education that flow from its increasing integration within the school system appear to have been reproduced at even greater intensity in the youth sector. First, young people tend to be less mobile and far more dependent upon public transport than those who attend evening classes,[56] so that the

concentration of facilities upon one large campus may effectively exclude large numbers of young people from regular attendance even
though they may live within the catchment area of the school. Particularly in rural and suburban areas this leads to a grossly uneven distribution of capital resources. In urban areas where the facilities may be
more accessible they tend however to be dominated by groups of young
people drawn from a particular locale, or social or ethnic group. As
Eggleston found in his survey of patterns of youth club affiliation it
is very rare for a centre or unit to comprehensively serve the needs of
young people resident in a given community or locality, for whatever
their base of operations they almost invariably tend to: 'both reinforce
and perpetuate the social status and social interaction patterns of the
adult community.'[57] The concentration of resources upon a single
campus within a given area thus tends to engender additional inequalities
in the allocation of provision and covert discrimination that may well
exacerbate existing divisions and tensions within both the school and
the wider community. This is a factor that is particularly, but not
exclusively, significant in racially mixed areas where the youth club
becomes defined as the territory of one particular group, a canvas for
the expression of a collective identity: 'Black young people see youth
clubs less as clubs in the traditional sense, much more as territory within which they can express cultural preferences and political options.'[58]
Certainly the multi-racial community school appears to have been no
more successful in creating multi-racial youth clubs than free-standing
units,[59] any more than it has been able to prevent school-based clubs
becoming in other areas the social preserve of one particular group such
as the 'Rockers', 'Punks' or a district gang. It is in a racial context however that the lines of demarcation are most easily discernible and the
trend continues apparently unabated for minorities to demand 'de facto
separate racial provision . . . and the creation of "self-help" groups'.[60] As
Hill notes: 'Black teenagers . . . want their own youth clubs. Not only
that. If coloured membership increases in clubs which start off multi-
racial, the white teenagers often leave. Otherwise they don't join at all.'[61]
    Second, the facilities of the youth club or youth wing attached to a
school are largely pre-determined by the physical environment of the
school and the necessity to negotiate the distribution of these given
resources with other groups of users. As the manager of one school-
based youth centre explains:[62]

> There is one . . . major drawback in the design of these social areas
> of this centre. The policy of the centre (Shadsworth, Blackburn),

which developed as the design stage passed, is one of multi-use, or to be more specific, open access for the whole community with something for everyone. With such a policy the fact that the social areas are open plan means that they can be swamped by youths leaving little or no space, quiet or otherwise, for adults. While meetings and some table games could be held in the new sixth form teaching areas, the accommodation, with the exception of the craft block, looks like classrooms, even though it is more informal than at Carlton (a similar centre in Nottinghamshire). The youth tutor reports that youth are loath to use these areas. Certainly they are not attractive to youths especially in the working class area where considerable antipathy to school can exist.

The problems experienced at Shadsworth are certainly not unique, in similar units it has been necessary to institute separate entrances for different groups of clients, to lock through doors, specify alternative evenings and generally make every effort to keep certain groups at arm's length from each other. The hoped-for integration of youth facilities into the overall pattern of community provision has simply not materialized, shared premises patently do not of themselves initiate shared leisure. The types of activities engaged upon by those attending an evening centre or adult education class and those enjoyed by young people affiliated to a youth club tend to be as disparate as the behavioural norms prevalent in the respective groups. The result of this divide has been that community educators employed in community schools have been obliged to adopt forms of practice that have thwarted the good intentions of planners, architects and local authority officials, proving by their style of management that age and social divisions which are generic to society cannot be left neatly packaged at the school gates for collection at the end of the evening but will tend to re-assert themselves within the artificial atmosphere of the community school or centre.

As Haworth indicated, youth workers operating in shared or integrated school premises find, as do their colleagues in non-vocational adult education, that those individuals who found school unattractive or who were adjudged unsuccessful according to the criterion of the school, tend to be unwilling to return to that locale[63] even when it is superficially operating 'under new management'. As one survey found in this respect: 'only 38 per cent of the early leavers, who went to schools which provided clubs went to them, compared with 59 per cent of the later school leavers of the same age.'[64] Bristow describes the experience of one leader-teacher who reported that:[65]

An extreme difficulty in encouraging younger membership has been noticeable since the secondary school in the catchment area took over the premises as an annexe. It seems they are too much aware of school connotations as they see too much of the premises during the day under the wrong conditions.

The growth in school-based youth work since 1960 makes it increasingly unlikely that the Youth Service will have sufficient resources available to perform the role that Webb saw as its primary function; in his own words, 'the education production line has its refuse; that's where the Youth Service comes in'.[66] Webb envisages that the Youth Service might operate as a safety net capable of providing on a national scale an informal social education for those young people who either recoil from or are rejected by the school system. However, to perform this function effectively the Youth Service would not only require a sizeable increase in its budget but also to distance itself from the schools, establishing a parallel non-school network of provision. Failure to adopt such a policy and curb the drift to a school-dominated service will in all probability result in the Youth Service catering for fewer and fewer of those young people who in Webb's opinion are in most need of its expertise and help. This is a view that is endorsed by Parry and Flowers, who found that:[67]

those who reject education tend also to reject the Youth Service. Any further identification of the Service with the school, such as utilising school premises for youth work will tend to create a greater rift between the Service and children in the lowest socio-economic groups.

The danger of the Youth Service acquiring a narrower class base as a result of growing integration with the school system may be the most widely debated aspect of this tendency but it is not the only cause for concern. Equally disturbing, but rarely discussed, may well be the impact that these units have upon the young people who outwardly are the most fully integrated participant members of the school community. Many of these institutions can now claim to provide an almost total environment for the young person, one in which their working day is regulated by the school timetable and their evening and weekend leisure activities are organized by the youth tutor and his or her staff. A number of the community schools even provide evening meals for their pupils to save them an 'unnecessary' journey home for food. This may be very laudable, but if, as Simpson claims, 'one of the goals of education is to stimulate pupils' activity outside the school walls',[68] then these institutions may well be offering a service of questionable value by encouraging young people to remain in an abnormal and 'essentially a contrived and controlled environment',[69] that hinders rather than encourages self-realization.

Schools, not least those labelled 'community', remain monolithic organizations in which it is virtually a condition of attendance that the consumer, pupil or adult, accepts a subservient role.[70] The largely unchallenged norm being 'that the head is in charge of the whole complex',[71] even though such a concentration of power in the hands of one individual may be 'increasingly at variance with prevailing social custom'.[72] The expansion of the school into areas of leisure activity previously outside its orbit can only lead to a reduction in the individual pupil's control over their social environment. Young people may be encouraged to increasingly 'perceive the social system as "given", unaware that the opportunity to re-define it is open to them, and, that having taken it they may construct a new social reality in which they are participants rather than receivers.'[73]

As Williams has noted, schools may be excellent institutions for reproducing the existing social order, but with few notable exceptions they are either unwilling or incapable of equipping their pupils with the skills that will enable them to become full members 'of an educated and participatory democracy'.[74] A role they are unlikely to perform as long as the management structure of the school is formulated to ensure that 'in contrast to other normative organisations, it is functional for instrumental elites to subordinate expressive ones.'[75] The institutional structure of the school is in itself a powerful instructional agent that can inculcate in its pupils a fear of freedom and encourage a retreat into the alternative culture of adolescence.[76] The result is, as Noble found, that many young people may exhibit a marked reluctance to assume adult roles, even when these are freely offered. 'We have tried hard to encourage keen members to participate in all decisions made, but it has proved difficult. They prefer, and have been conditioned to expect, to have decisions made for them by others.'[77]

Noble was writing of his experience of working with unattached groups of young people where it was relatively easy for him to transfer decision-making responsibilites to the client group. For youth workers employed in community schools and the larger free-standing centres such an option is a less realistic one, for they are obliged to manage a plant that is 'too costly and precious to be handed over to young people'.[78] The bigger the unit, the wider the spread of client groups and the more substantive the managerial structure,[79] so the more circumscribed are the policy options available to the youth worker and the fewer the opportunities whereby he or she might delegate power to their clients. The growing integration in many areas of the Youth Service within the school system can only reduce rather than improve the prospects of the Youth Service transforming itself into an organization wherein the young 'learn the democratic process'.[80] The introduction of an additional tier of management that interjects the head-teacher or principal of the community school as a control agent mediating between the youth tutor and the area youth officer can only lead to the creation of a further barrier to the realistic involvement of clients in the decision making process. Traditionally the powers of the head-teachers are such that they can only impinge further upon the professional autonomy of the youth worker and his or her freedom to adopt any style of leadership that they deem appropriate. For example the head-teacher of one school determined before even the youth wing was built 'that it would have to concentrate on constructive activity'.[81] The head-teacher role, unlike that of a management committee which tends to convene infrequently, or that of an area youth officer who will rarely choose to involve himself in an active supervisory role, is a constant managerial factor and one which traditionally represents a hierarchical and monocratic approach; one that is 'astonishing in its degree of autonomy'[82] and which the youth worker could only challenge at his peril.

The relationship between the school and the youth wing, and between the head and the youth tutor, despite many superficial similarities, is not strictly analogous to that which prevails between the head and the classroom teacher. In part this divergence can be the direct result of an LEA policy which imposes a youth wing or club upon a reluctant or indifferent head-teacher making it difficult for an effective working partnership to mature; as Phelan asks in relation to this problem:[83]

> How far is it reasonable for some LEAs to put youth work and formal education side by side, with a youth tutor post, accompanied by a brief explanation as to the raison d'être for this, and then step back and leave events to take their course? What is important, and what must be seriously questioned on the evidence of this survey is whether sufficient dialogue has taken place – in some cases – between the school and the LEA as to the purpose and the potential of these posts.

The result of this failure in communication has been as Phelan later concludes: 'that the traditional division and separate functions of school and youth work are being perpetuated in a disguised form.'[84]

Better communications and more precise job descriptions will not in themselves solve irreconcilable differences that are often rooted in the traditional tendency of formal education and youth work to be seen as separate fields of endeavour, by many observers and practitioners alike.[85] Not surprisingly many youth tutors come to perceive themselves to be confronted with often incompatible, as well as ill-defined, role expectations. Both part of, yet external to, the school; school-teacher, youth leader and community worker at one and the same time, serving the school, club members and the wider community, or at least those elements of it which are capable or anxious to exert pressure upon him. In the words of one such youth leader:[86]

> You are pulled so many ways. Obviously the Warden (head of the community school) pulls you mostly and then secondly you've got the members to play ball with, and finally the people you meet in the community. Probably thirdly there's your Area Further Education Advisor and officials from County Hall. So there's always for me a big decision as to how far I will go to satisfy all those interests.

It is not sufficient to explain the depth of such role conflicts in terms of the pathology of the individual staff member, because as Venables clearly showed in her study, in attitudinal terms no 'noteworthy differences existed between the three groups – heads, teachers and youth workers. Thus on the evidence of this study, it must be inferred that the differences that do occur between the groups are likely to be environmental rather than inherent.'[87] The root causes of the role conflict appear, as Venables indicated, to be found in the nature of the job itself. Even though the youth tutor may embody both the roles of teacher and youth worker he or she does so at separate times and the ill-defined terms of reference can reproduce, and indeed often exaggerate, the distance between them, a distance which has 'tended to make the relationship between teachers and youth workers a competitive rather than a co-operative one and (in which) mutual ignorance leads to biased appraisals.'[88] The youth tutor internalizes these contradictions, but in doing so does not eliminate them, rather within the school environment he or she personifies them. The youth tutor is a hybrid suspected by other youth workers as somehow less than a professional, and by other teachers is often viewed as a threat to the stability of the school and to the established patterns of staff-pupil interaction. He or she is in consequence driven to the periphery of school life. The role becomes defined as marginal to the main pursuits of the school, a marginality that is often implied and reinforced by the type of children that the youth tutor is designated to work with both in the classroom and in the club, those euphemistically called the ROSLA group, the non-examination fifth and so on.

The marginality of the youth tutor to the community school structure is also expressed in the transient nature of the appointment itself. Elias, for example, describes one LEA that takes positive steps to restrict the working life of its youth tutors to approximately three years by offering them preferential treatment in terms of secondment that will qualify them for alternative appointments or promotion.[89] This built-in obsolescence, almost unique in the educational sphere, expresses in tangible form a recognition on the part of the LEA of the exceptional pressures exerted upon the youth tutor in his working environment, but significantly it also re-affirms his or her marginality to the school. He or she is judged not to require the long-term relationships within either the school or the community that could be expected to grow over a longer period of time. The cumulative effect is such that whatever the salary scale[90] or titular position given the post by the LEA, the youth tutor is obliged to hold down a post where 'the incumbent is seen as a junior member of the staff'.[91] As a consequence of this the youth tutor is in a weak position in any conflict situation, particularly where this relates to the advocacy of a client's case against the entrenched power structure of the school, founded upon a low status post and susceptible to pressure from forces both within and without the school, the youth tutor has little real room for manoeuvre. Safety therefore lies for many youth tutors in a narrow definition of their role; one that obviates many of the assumed youth worker functions, in the words of one teacher-youth worker: 'Youth tutors should really be just teachers in out of school activities, which has very little to do with the overall purpose of youth work. At least then there is no danger of upsetting the school.'[92]

Hayman may well be correct when he says that youth tutors do very little youth work in the normally accepted meaning of the term, however that is not, and never has been, their sole function. They are usually part of a community education team whose purpose is to develop an integrated educational programme that ensures there is, in the words of Henry Morris, 'no leaving school – the child would enter at three and leave the college only in extreme old age'.[93] Within this paradigm the youth wing or club run by the youth tutor and integrated within the community school takes on a quite unique youth work function: that of providing a staging post which bridges the gap for those not proceeding to higher education, between formal and informal education, between the compulsory and the voluntary. Any evaluation of school based youth work in a community school setting must therefore take into account its effectiveness in performing this role.

The available evidence indicates that the hoped for element of continuity is absent in the community schools. Elias saw a distinct demarcation line, drawn according to class criteria, between the clients of the youth clubs and those of the adult education sector in the schools he studied. This was a common phenomenon, but the variable lay in the extent to which this division was the direct consequence of staff planning, for in a number of community schools he investigated: 'tutors deliberately went out of their way to help the type of young person that caused concern to adult users.'[94] Given the low, almost non-existent take-up by working-class adults of non-vocational educational facilities in community schools,[95] the policy adopted by the youth tutors described in Elias's study does not appear to have paid dividends in terms of life-long affiliation. Particularly discouraging in this respect have been the findings of Mayes, who in his detailed study of adolescent enrolment in the adult classes held at one community school over a four-year period dating from the inauguration of the college to the end of the academic year 1972-3, found that from a peak of 13 per cent of total enrolments during the initial year the adolescent take-up declined sharply to a nominal 4 per cent in 1972-3, a fall-off that prompted his comment: 'the trend towards pupil and ex-pupil participation in adult education provision is not a feature of the Leicestershire Community Colleges.'[96]

The findings of Mayes endorse those of Palfrey and Thomas whose more ambitious research indicated that:[97]

> senior pupils in secondary schools also providing accommodation for adult education classes know very little about the nature of these classes. The notion that 'community colleges' is equivalent to 'night school' is entrenched in the adolescent's conception of evening classes. The more 'academic' pupils (i.e. in this study those in grammar schools) share with the less 'academic' (secondary modern pupils) a similar level of ignorance about what is often termed 'other further education'. Attendance at a youth club does not lead to an added interest in what many adult educationalists hope will be a natural progression from youth to adult activities . . . . Although youth club and community college members are neighbours in the same premises, their fields of activity remain apart.

Such divergence has even been recorded amongst adolescents using an integrated sports and community centre. The survey found that:[98]

two distinct and separate sub-cultures existed. There was little, or no, rapport between the two groups of members. Sports members were content to stay in the Sports area and apparently saw nothing to attract them to the Community area. Further there was limited opportunity for either group to interact with leaders from the other area: thus Community leaders, for instance, were not well known to sports users . . . . Differences were such that many members could see for themselves – 'Its the brainy ones that go downstairs (Sports area), the ones up here are all mental', remarked a seventeen year-old girl in the Community area.

In the light of the available empirical evidence the advocacy of inte-grated school, youth and adult provision on the grounds that it will help to promote life-long client affiliation seems to be ill-founded. Economically the case for joint provision may well be sound but in educational terms the investment appears to have been far less successful than expected. For many LEAs the commitment to integrated school and youth provision represents, in both physical and intellectual terms, such a substantial investment that whatever the levels of success they are irreversible, for the funding is simply not available to create an alter-native structure capable of meeting the needs of those who reject school-based provision. The Community schools, like the 'Withywood Centres' simply 'tie up the bulk of the available money',[99] devouring resources at roughly the same rate whether they are empty or full. They do how-ever possess one undoubted advantage over the free-standing youth centre, their facilities are easily adaptable for school use offering suit-able 'social accommodation for older pupils'.[100] The staff likewise can be fully utilized, providing discos and leisure activities for the younger pupils, running the Careers Department, co-ordinating outdoor pursuits, supervising community work options and the like within the school. The problems are thus at one level eminently manageable; the only one that lingers is the one that has existed since before Albemarle, namely what precisely should the LEAs do in order to provide a reasonably comprehensive service for young people in their area.

5　Spreading the load

The expansion that took place in the Youth Service during the post-Albemarle period and which entailed the investment of 'something in excess of £50 million . . . (in) . . . purpose built plant',[1] does not appear to have led to any significant increase in the proportion of young people affiliated to youth clubs and youth organizations. Albemarle and related central and local government initiatives may have achieved a measure of success by arresting the decline that had been a feature of the 1950s, but these initiatives do not seem to have reduced the percentage of those young persons designated by Albemarle as the 'unclubbables', or to have reversed the trend for rates of affiliation to fall off radically amongst those aged sixteen and over. Indeed many commentators, on the basis of admittedly limited research, believe this drift has become more rather than less pronounced since 1960.[2]

The Fairbairn-Milson Report, published nearly a decade after Albemarle, certainly based its recommendations upon research findings which indicated that the clientele of the Youth Service was being drawn increasingly from amongst those at the lower end of the statutory age range, and that overall the percentage of young people attached to the Youth Service was diminishing.[3] Fairbairn-Milson saw the statutory age range which commenced at fourteen as being anachronistic, recognizing as a subsequent study confirmed that 'the highest proportion of young people on the streets . . . are in the twelve to thirteen age range'.[4] Given this state of affairs it seemed indisputable that some form of leisure provision should be made available for those below fourteen, so why not use the often under-utilized facilities of the Youth Service and the undoubted expertise of its staff. Also as the voluntary youth organizations, particularly the uniformed groups, who were accepted as an integral part of the Youth Service and who received grant-aid accordingly, both from the DES and individual LEAs, were attracting an ever greater proportion of their membership from amongst those aged fourteen and below,[5] it was administratively an unrealistic line of demarcation anyway. The solution therefore, according to Fairbairn-Milson, was to recognize the new situation and legislate for it accordingly: 'Work amongst the younger age groups should be mainly the responsibility of the schools and the voluntary organisations . . . (and) . . . that the existing lower age limit of fourteen should disappear.'[6] To cater for those young people who were either 'unattached' or who no longer found the existing provision attractive or relevant it was recommended that a new Youth and Community Service should be created; one that would be capable of meeting 'the needs of young people by making contact with them wherever they are to be found'.[7]

The 'Youth and Community Work in the 70s' Report correctly acknowledged that it was not within the capability of the Youth Service to attract those young people aged sixteen and over who had already deserted them back into either the youth clubs or the existing voluntary groups in any appreciable numbers. They had either to be abandoned and left to their own devices, a state of affairs that for the vast majority of them appeared to create no insurmountable difficulties and induce few traumas, or alternatively, new radically different forms of provision had to be sought if contact was to be maintained or established.

From the mid-1960s onwards a number of experimental projects were initiated;[8] these were designed primarily to cater for the so-called 'unclubbables' who were described by Ince in a report of one such project as those young people with:[9]

> no interest in the Youth Service and the facilities it offered. This was not really because the service failed to give them what they wanted, or in the way they wanted it, in fact many of the facilities wanted by the young people were already being provided by existing youth clubs. But they appeared to reject the youth clubs because they either disliked what they considered to be the autocratic structure of the Youth Service or because traditionally they did not like the idea of joining or of being a member of any kind of organisation. Many young people also had an almost pervasive fear of anything or anybody new. So for these young people to go to a youth club where they might not recognise the other people there, was too great an ordeal. They much preferred to stay in the 'safety' of the streets, secure in their little group of friends and acquaintances. There was also, amongst many of the young people over fifteen years of age, an almost total rejection of the Youth Service merely because they associated it with school and childhood. For these young people, the public house appeared to symbolise freedom and adulthood, and it was for them the focus of their leisure time and attention.

The majority of the unattached however shared few of the characteristics of the young people described by Ince. For as Parry and Flowers discovered, the non-affiliated were overwhelmingly made up of those who had sampled the facilities offered by the Youth Service and found them wanting:[10]

> The failure of large numbers of children to participate in clubs, groups and organisations was not because they did not know about them, or because they had no experience of them – 92 per cent of children had been a member of at least one such club or group at some time between the ages of seven and fifteen years.

These findings are confirmed by both Bone and Ross[11] and Eggleston.[12] Eggleston also found that even amongst young people who were strongly committed to a particular group or club the norm was to 'shop around', sampling other clubs and organizations before opting to either join or abstain from membership. Thus it may be deduced that the authentic 'unclubbables' described by Ince probably amount to less than 8 per cent, of whom only a percentage are the 'disadvantaged adolescents'[13] and 'at risk' individuals who have tended to attract the concentrated attention of the majority of unattached youth work projects. All the existing evidence indicates that the unattached 70 per cent are not isolated from the Youth Service due to their own innate inadequacies, but overwhelmingly because having experienced what it has to offer they conclude that the benefits accruing from membership are not commensurate with the cost in time, effort or expense that is entailed. The statutory sector of the Youth Service partly as a result of its own structure and its past emphasis upon the construction of a network of youth centres and youth wings may well have encouraged, as much as any other agency, the development of a style of provision that is in the main 'only interested in those who are prepared to come on to the premises'.[14]

A fairly widespread reaction to the dominance of the centre orientated approach to youth work has been the emergence of independent projects based upon voluntary work and community development schemes,[15] and the use of unattached workers by both statutory and voluntary agencies. These it was hoped would make 'contact' with young people 'wherever they are to be found'. The remit of these unattached workers, both full and part-time was:[16]

> (i) to make contact with young people individually or in groups, who are not reached effectively by society's usual socialising agencies; schools, youth clubs, etc.
> (ii) to negotiate with such agencies on their behalf or to provide

alternative resources to help to meet the social and recreative needs of these young people.

(iii) to develop relationships with such young people which may create for them situations in which they become better equipped to cope with society and its institutions.

(iv) to help young people to develop the social maturity that will enable them to grow independent of the support of the worker, and then develop into mature responsible adults.

Although handicapped by an almost total lack of workers trained for this specialist type of intervention, unattached work seemed to offer a number of positive advantages. First, it helped the Youth Service to establish contact with groups of young people with whom it had previously had only minimal contact:[17]

The Authority's detached youth workers have shown an ability to reach, make contact with, and form working relationships with, a variety of groups of young people. Most of these young people have not been reached effectively by other forms of youth work.

Second, it was an intervention that entailed low unit costs. The unattached workers demand no investment in expensive buildings, or the employment of support staff such as secretaries or caretakers.

Despite these advantages, detached youth work has not expanded at the rate that might have been predicted in the 1960s. Currently, according to Marks, 5 per cent of all full-time youth workers are employed on unattached work,[18] and a total of 48 LEAs finance unattached youth work projects.[19] The number of workers engaged in this area does not appear to be increasing and may well be declining, for economic cut-backs have tended to disproportionately affect this area of work. As inflation has gathered momentum, so the maintenance costs and salary bills for the existing youth provision have risen and LEAs have been obliged to make economies. They can hardly justify the closure of an established centre or club, particularly when this represents a substantial financial investment and is also in all probability managed by a committee made up, in part at least, of influential local political and social personalities. If cutbacks and trimming are called for, the LEA will often therefore find it easier to run down the more anonymous unattached project, a solution that is usually made far more feasible by the high turnover in staff employed on such projects. Their post being simply frozen upon the resignation of the incumbent or where the project is of an experimental nature then the contracts are not renewed when the current phase ends.

Given the small number of workers employed on unattached work, the majority of whom are employed on a full-time basis, it is inevitable that few young people meet, let alone have regular contact with, a detached worker. As an approach to youth work however it has had a considerable impact upon the Youth Service in general, for it has:[20]

> tended to reveal more problems than it solved and any success depended upon close co-operation from a wide range of personnel in the social, educational and medical services.

The theoretical input gained from the unattached projects has been a bonus that has given many youth workers and administrators a valuable insight into their own performance, and which has encouraged them to greater cognizance of the world of young people that exists beyond the confines of the youth club. It has led many to move away[21]

> from the idea that it is 'normal' to belong to a club or group and from attempts to 'socialise' and 'dealienate' the so-called 'unclub-bables' through leisure and sporting activities.

The fiscal limitations placed upon LEAs in recent years have severely curtailed the ability of the statutory sector to embark upon experimental youth work projects. Consequently, other agencies, both statutory and voluntary, have played a progressively more active role in certain areas of youth work most notably in connection with interventions aimed at those youth persons who might be designated as socially, culturally and/or economically deprived. These interventions have been in part based upon an acknowledgment that:[22]

> a cost conscious policy which sets out to provide a service through modern management techniques and a maximum use of existing resources and premises such as school buildings is likely to confirm the exclusion of the most under-privileged working class boys and girls whom the Youth Service was originally designed to attract.

If the mainstream Youth Service has been unable or unwilling to transfer resources from established commitments in order to cater for this group of young people then various *ad hoc* groups, voluntary welfare agencies and, significantly, other national and local governmental departments, have increasingly been, for a variety of reasons, prepared to do so.

The Children's and Young Person's Act (1969), provided a considerable impetus for this type of intervention with its introduction of 'Intermediate Treatment' for offenders aged twelve to seventeen. Managed by local authority social service departments, it was originally envisaged that the scheme would largely operate through the auspices of the established youth groups. However, the reaction of those groups to the scheme was by no means a universally favourable one, varying from downright hostility, through graduations of benign indifference to sympathetic interest. The opposition to IT forcibly expressed by one full-time youth leader who was also significantly a serving JP was not uncommon:[23]

> What I am against is the idea of the Youth Service being used as an instrument of punishment – whether we like it or not this is precisely what Intermediate Treatment means. I cannot see any good coming from it at all . . . for the whole principle of voluntary attendance is brought into question.

This attitude was not a universally held one, for many youth workers welcomed IT as an extension and formalization of a previously informal linkage that existed between individuals working in the Probation Service, Children's Departments and sympathetic youth workers. As one Scout Commissioner explained in whole-heartedly welcoming the scheme:[24]

> I think the philosophy of Intermediate Treatment . . . runs parallel to those of the Scout Movement, i.e. new experiments, challenge, opportunities for achievement, associations with other people in a fairly structured but fluid setting. I think our type of programme, from outdoor-based activities, to hobbies and community service activities all follow this philosophy.

This enthusiasm was echoed by the NABC. As early as 1968 they had in co-operation with thirty-eight Local Authorities been operating a pilot scheme involving approximately 500 boys who had been attached to NABC units and activity groups under Fit Persons (later Care) Orders. Following the introduction of IT the NABC appointed two full-time field officers whose brief was to encourage the development of IT schemes amongst affiliated groups.[25] However, in general the response to the Youth Service could best be described as tepid, and significantly this is endorsed by an article published in 1977 which discusses in some detail ways in which the scheme might be developed and significantly the Youth Service does not even warrant a passing reference.[26] The failure to involve the Youth Service more fully in IT work to an extent reflected a suspicion on the part of many social workers that the established clubs and groups were unsuitable for their clients and that they were largely of a type that their clients had anyway already tried and found wanting. This led many social service departments to inaugurate their own independent IT groups. These groups were run either by social workers on a part-time basis or, as in Birmingham and Hertfordshire, by specially appointed youth social workers, as one recent survey notes: 'There is now a growing number of specialist I.T. workers, and the majority of the Social Service Departments in England have an I.T. Officer and/or full-time I.T. workers covering different areas of the authority.'[27]

Davies suggests that it was not solely scepticism on the part of the social workers as to the value and relevance of existing youth provision for their clients that led many of them to create an independent and often parallel structure. It was, he maintains, also a direct consequence of a frequently held belief amongst social workers that the full-time youth workers along with their part-time colleagues were 'unqualified' to effectively provide the group work and counselling inputs that the social workers deemed to be an integral part of IT.[28]

The social service department groups, once inaugurated, tended to grow apace particularly through the acquisition of a preventive role that complemented the original curative and punitive ones. For example, the young people who were legally obliged to attend an IT group have often been encouraged to bring along friends and brothers and sisters; whilst social workers who during the course of their generic work encounter young people whom they consider to be 'at risk' would use such groups as a resource. As a result: 'Children participating in I.T. schemes are largely non-offenders. Offenders brought before the court are increasingly being fined or discharged at one extreme or committed to borstal, detention centre or care at the other.'[29]

It was neither new nor revolutionary for social workers employed in the new social service departments to become involved in work with groups of young people or in community development schemes. Prior to Seebohm a great deal of such work was carried out by social workers employed in a variety of settings and particularly for those in the NCSS community schemes,[30] who started the first youth community project in Slough in 1938.[31] What was noteworthy after 1970 was the rapid growth in the sheer volume of such interventions, an expansion that reflected the belief of Seebohm that the social service departments should play a major part in the development of community identity, in mobilizing local resources, in organizing voluntary effort and in ensuring community participation.[32] Social workers and their community work colleagues are as a result of this orientation displaying a growing willingness to instigate wide-ranging youth work projects designed in part to overcome what they perceive as the inadequacies of both the statutory and voluntary youth work agencies.[33] This had led one commentator to warn that 'It would be easy for a dichotomy to occur between educationally-based youth work and social work based youth work.'[34]

Certainly where social workers are conceptually able to overcome the limitations of a casework approach founded upon a view that they are 'the agents of society who are entrusted with one aspect of the preservation and enforcement of a moral code,'[35] they appear to be able to offer young people, particularly those with special needs, a far more practical and realistic support service than most youth work agencies. The social service departments have the resources at their command to make a far more integrated and long-term intervention. They have no cut-off point at age twenty and can offer support not only to the client, but also to his or her family, and relate this intervention to the wider environmental setting. The last is often the crucial element, for as Bond notes, the social worker may have in many cases to accept from the onset that:[36]

> the clients problems are situationally based . . . (and) . . . try to convince those clients that there is nothing wrong with them and that they do not need supportive casework help. On the contrary, the casework must convince them that what they need is another house, more money, etc., that they have a right to those things and that there are ways of getting them.

In adopting this approach social workers will tend to find support from their working environment, for unlike statutory youth workers they are not seen as marginal appendages attached to a department that is overwhelmingly concerned with the management of schools and other educational institutions, that have only a superficial relationship with the activities of youth workers. Social workers particularly since the creation of social service departments are by training and background increasingly in organizational terms at least, integrated within their own departments where accordingly they are recognized as professionals or semi-professionals,[37] possessing distinctive skills. Social service departments may be faced with 'continued questioning' and demands for the redefinition of their work which has 'clearly affected the morale of the professionals working within them',[38] yet the morale of these professionals in part flows from the natural coterie of the department. It contrasts sharply with the predominately low self-image and public evaluation of the youth worker and his role, to quote from Watts and Whitworth:[39]

youth workers used as subjects thought 'the level' of their profession as low when they made comparisons with other professions . . . and that there is little or no public image of youth leadership. What did exist were 'low and misinformed' stereotypes – as one who keeps children off the streets, kind of scout-master, games organiser . . . . The public also thought the work a soft option.

Social work is also viewed as a long-term career commitment; youth work however is viewed by many, both employers and employees, as a fleeting affiliation, as the Director of the Community Development Trust explained: 'The life of a club leader is five years. After this he ought to move on. Instead of having an ageing Youth Service we should aim to achieve a rapid turnover.'[40]

In terms of professional status, long-term commitment and training social workers are thus far better equipped, and are indeed anxious to adopt a multi-dimensional approach, for as Thorpe points out: 'Ultimately, if social workers are to gain recognition as a profession, then they will have to produce tangible results on a large scale . . . which . . . caters for the totality of human needs.'[41] Youth workers can have no such incentive. Their existing canvas is too small, their powers of intervention so limited and their professional support so inadequate, that they are obliged for reasons of self-preservation back into the clubs and schools, and the often narrow counselling role that those institutions impose upon them.

Even within the context of the multi-dimensional approach social workers are obliged to make political decisions regarding the distribution of scarce resources between conflicting areas of need. It is an area of activity that is implicit in social work practice: 'In various agencies, professionals are involved in selecting from a large 'eligible population' a smaller number of 'appropriate clients.'[42] Such choices, for good or ill, are largely denied youth workers, for they can only effectively operate with the clientele they have, those, that is, who have freely chosen to frequent the club or centre, or make and maintain a social contact. Detached youth workers face a similar problem although obviously to a lesser extent as they can move their area of operation in order to avoid old clients or acquire new ones, but as Farrant and Marchant point out: 'the type of clients with whom he initially makes contact will, to a large extent, determine the future programme of work.'[43] Not surprisingly, the social service departments are proving, whatever their limitations, far more adaptable and effective in dealing with the immediate needs of deprived and isolated young people. By definition they are selective, the Youth Service is largely random.

Social service departments are not the only agencies to have shown a growing willingness to intervene in the sphere of youth provision. The Probation Service has involved itself in similar remedial and preventative work with older adolescents. This has been very much on an *ad hoc* basis, flowing from the recognition of a localized need or the possibility of a worthwhile preventative intervention. As Davies notes, his survey clearly showed that this type of work has been growing in recent years, for 'In addition to a continuing involvement in Intermediate Treatment most probation areas . . . organised activities for their clients ranging from trips to the local leisure park to a transatlantic voyage by yacht.'[44] Only a limited number of the clients of the Probation Service fall within the statutory age range of the Youth Service but it is upon the younger clients that much of the preventative work is concentrated. In Gateshead, for example, the Probation Service organizes a five-a-side football league in order that its clients may be 'drawn back into society' through involvement in a social setting with other young men whose 'only qualification for attending is an interest in sport and a willingness to turn up regularly'.[45]

Given the ratio of nine males to every one female committed for an indictable offence these activities have predictably been in the main sporting and outdoor pursuits, of the type that have traditionally been considered to be 'challenging' and 'character building'. Since the sponsorship of Community Service Orders by the Home Office under the terms of the Criminal Justice Act (1972),[46] the emphasis has however shifted away from the more physical pursuits and towards group work based upon philanthropic and altruistic community activities. The Youth Service has certainly benefitted from and contributed towards the scheme 'proving to be a most receptive group' regarding the assimilation of CSO volunteers.[47] In Nottinghamshire where the majority of the offenders in the pilot scheme were aged seventeen to twenty-five, 9 per cent (27 out of 300) of the offenders in the first year were placed as assistant leaders in youth clubs.[48] It is perhaps not insignificant that the Youth Service appears to have been a far more effective partner in the CSO scheme, where it is offering adults and older adolescents the chance to perform a leadership function, than in the IT scheme where it is required to provide an educative experience for the younger offender cum member. Little integration has taken place between the various schemes and this has given added weight to the warning of the Seebohm Report that: 'Recent developments in aftercare and parole bring the probation and aftercare service increasingly into work in the community and thus raise the danger of unplanned overlapping.'[49]

Sadly the Youth Service appears too weak to provide such co-ordination.

Local Authority Recreation and Leisure Departments have shown a growing propensity to take responsibility for areas of work that might previously have been considered to be the prerogative of the various constituent parts of the Youth Service.[50] The recreation departments have set up play schemes, adventure play groups, play buses, summer holiday centres and generally extended the concept of the 'playground' until in many areas it bears only the most superficial resemblance to the handful of swings and roundabouts dotted about a flat expanse of dull tarmac of days gone by. The employment of full-time trained staff, supplemented in many areas by the large-scale recruitment of young people via the Job Creation Programme has meant that in urban areas this sector has in terms of staff been the fastest growing in recent years.[51] Certainly the age range of the young people involved in the projects managed by recreation departments has tended to widen out across the age spectrum as new schemes have been developed that are designed to cater for older adolescents, notably the long-term un-employed and the persistent truant.

The composite picture that begins to emerge is not one of rational, even development during the last decade, but of pragmatic *ad hoc* augmentations with a corresponding blurring of the divisions relating to departmental and agency areas of concern. However, it may be possible to construct a limited *de facto* division of areas of responsibil-ity, both at a national and local level. The DES and the LEAs appear to be restricting their interest to the development of educationally based youth work, the servicing of clubs and the support and integration of the various voluntary organizations, although the DES recently tried unsuccessfully to jettison its responsibility for grant-aiding voluntary organizations building projects.[52] This leaves community service projects for young people to the Home Office for funding through Urban Aid, and the DHSS and local social service departments to supervise and finance work amongst the 'youth at risk'. The Ministry of Defence is also involved through its support of the cadet corps and the service youth teams. Even the Foreign Office plays a part via its funding of the somewhat misleadingly titled British Youth Council. It is a body that in no way can claim to represent the grass-roots of the Youth Service, there being, in fact, no mechanism whereby its officers can be elected or called to account by the members of the various groups that form the Youth Service. It is, in the words of a *Times Educational Supple-ment* editorial, merely: 'an apparatus for already aspiring politicians provisioned . . . to provide a British youth presence at international conferences.'[53]

No formalized structure exists to co-ordinate or even encourage co-operation between these various agencies at either a national or local level. Obviously projects are initiated that straddle the agency boundaries,[54] and a number of these have emerged to national prominence, for example, 'After Six' and 'Springboard'.

'After Six' in particular illustrates how such agency collaboration emerges from isolated individual initiatives, and how it can grow to involve organizations that might normally be considered as being outside the 'orbit' of the Youth Service. 'After Six' grew out of the concern felt by a number of probation officers over the plight of the actual and potential young homeless in London. Initially it comprised of a very limited scheme offering temporary 'crash' accommodation to young people whom the organizers felt to be 'at risk'. This grew rapidly as the scheme itself exposed the extent of the latent demand. Within fourteen months it had grown into a round-the-clock information and housing aid service, employing three full-time staff whose salaries are paid for by grants from eight local authority housing committees and the GLC, and ten full-time volunteers. In 1975 it co-ordinated a nationwide campaign designed to make young people in the provinces aware of the particular difficulties entailed in moving to London without sufficient funds and forethought.[55]

'Springboard', established in Sunderland in 1975, is another joint project and is one that is likely to set a pattern that will be replicated in many parts of the country. Within three years it has grown into the largest job creation scheme in Britain and the biggest single employer of young people engaged upon full-time paid social and community work. Designed to 'provide worthwhile temporary work in the field of personal social services',[56] it was first proposed following a feasibility study carried out by the Sunderland Social Service Department and was then set up by the Community Service Volunteers who have managed the scheme since its inception in December 1975.

'Springboard' represents an example of the type of projects that may well emerge from the growing involvement of the Manpower Services Commission (MSC) in 'youth-work type' ventures. The MSC plans to spend over £14 million (at 1976 prices) during the next twelve months on community service schemes, plus a proportion of the £8.5 milion set aside for 'capital contribution' and of the £2.6 million designated for staff in local areas, on this type of provision. Thus, although the MSC is primarily concerned with matters relating to economic and manpower needs, it appears, whether it likes it or not, to be on the verge of becoming involved in the social education of the young. The impact of the amount of money it intends to spend cannot fail to seriously influence future Youth Service policy decisions, and although it is far too early to predict the outcome of the growing involvement of the MSC it does not seem premature to talk of a new partner joining those already in the field.

'After Six' and 'Springboard', except in terms of their size and budgets, are typical of many initiatives that have taken place in recent years, with often only the most limited reference to those agencies that are usually deemed to comprise the mainstream Youth Service. These have been in the main the end product of isolated, often individualistic attempts to solve local problems or national problems on a local basis. Where these responses are effective they are often remarkably so, but they often require a degree of agency co-operation that is absent in many, if not most areas. As Davies found: 'Even when collaboration actually works . . . on the ground, and that would seem to be comparatively rarely, it leaves many questions, especially about purpose unanswered.'[57] Far too many projects reflect the interests and needs of the organizers with often little real consideration being given to potential demand or client needs. This, however, is not the main problem which remains namely the reluctance of agencies, to integrate resources. As Bacon, the Senior Intermediate Treatment Officer of the NACB, has recently noted, 'the desire to co-operate is missing',[58] and as Tweedie found in his survey on youth provision in one area of Cumbria: 'Very little co-ordination was found to exist between the various agencies which are concerned with young people.'[59]

The appointment by Liverpool Authority's Chief Executive's Office of a Youth Affairs Co-ordinator may well prove to be a partial solution to the growing fragmentation of provision particularly of the type that operates on the periphery of the established Youth Service. It is a solution that hopefully will not curb the enthusiasm of those engaged in offering independent community provision, but will engender the cross-agency dialogue, the absence of which Nixon felt to be so damaging: 'Schools social work departments and youth and community workers will one day discover that they are all working with the same youngsters. Until that day the losers will always be the children.'[60]

It is probably premature to talk of the Youth Service entering into its 'community phase' as Eggleston maintains,[61] for the growth that has taken place in this area has been both uneven and spasmodic, but substantial shifts have taken place. 'The building of independent statutory units has almost ceased'[62] and although the growth in the school-based sector shows little sign of losing momentum, it is likely that if the Youth Service is to avoid either stagnation or contraction then it is only in the area of community-based work that salvation will be found.

Conclusion

It has long been an integral part of the folk wisdom of the Youth Service that it is an organization in a state of perpetual change: 'Because young people use the Service on a voluntary basis and can leave us when what we offer is not longer relevant, constant reappraisal will always be part of the agony of the Youth Service.'[1] According to such a model, the Youth Service might be considered the very paradigm of flexibility, ready to tack this way and then that according to the changing demands of both clients and society alike. Administrators are often at pains to explain that they are obliged to continually restructure both the type and style of provision offered young people, as one LEA policy document explains: 'The nature of the Youth Service in a rapidly changing society is such that its aims and methods do need reappraisal at intervals not longer than four or five years.'[2]

As a direct consequence of this belief the literature of the Youth Service abounds with documents and reports, articles and statements on the future of the Youth Service, the role of the Youth Service and so forth. In reality, it is arguable that these tend to signify less a propensity for change and regeneration and more an uncertainty about the present; pipe-dreams about the future which serve to obscure the absence of a coherent contemporary philosophy and acceptable common role. Analysis of current practice inevitably invokes self-criticism and is likely to threaten the fragile consensus that serves to bind the disparate wings of the Youth Service together, therefore it tends to be avoided. Formulating plans for the future, especially when all parties know that they will invariably founder through a combination of a paucity of funds, governmental indifference and the duplicity of LEAs, is thus a safe and harmless way of generating self-activity and professional kudos. Behind the rhetoric and grandiloquent hopes for the future lies the reality of a service remarkable not for its dynamism and adaptability but for its innate conservatism, a conservatism rooted upon a structure which has shown itself capable of ensuring that 'the Establishment and voluntary organizations can combine to ossify the service by resisting change and hogging the available funds.'[3] Given this state of affairs it is not surprising, as Ette notes, that: 'As one moves and looks around the country it

100

is still unusual to see significant and imaginative Youth Service enterprise. Buildings are largely traditional and economical and thin on the ground.'[4]

The problem is, however, not purely one of plant or administration but is overwhelmingly structural. The Youth Service has been since 1870 and remains today primarily a 'leisure facility service',[5] yet, for reasons one suspects of self-image, it defines itself as a service primarily engaged in providing informal social education. This entails a definition of education that is so all-embracing, imprecise and conceptually loose that it can be used to justify almost any activity which the Youth Service chooses to offer its clients – from a visit to the pub, to a game of bingo or ping-pong. Combined with such concepts as client self-direction and non-judgmentalism which are themselves rarely quantified but often discussed, the initial educational stance tends to emerge as little more than a rationalization and justification for the use of well-tried techniques of social control developed to keep the 'kids happy'.[6] Almost universally the intellectual content of youth work is close to what Russians call *Meshchantsvo* – petty, null philistinism, a veritable bingo substitute that 'expresses nothing about the people who consume it but their deprivation'.[7]

Apart from its cheapness, the justification for this type of provision is not difficult to ascertain, for it is basically inspired by a desire to produce conformity. It is, to quote Ewen:[8]

a kindly device to contain the young until they have the 'good sense' to recognise the value of that which is. It must therefore be largely about play, like the bread and circuses of ancient Rome. It must above all things avoid such issues as 'politics', as 'race', as 'poverty', for as long as the young are happy with their five-a-side and their discotheques, they are nice young people; not like hairy students breathing revolution around every cloister corner. So we devise a Youth Service which reflects the beer and bingo conformity of our safe society. Even when the kids are unemployed, we offer the day-time opening of the youth club, so that they can play snooker or ping-pong, in case they get into mischief or vent their anger at the odd lamp-post.

Given its bill of fare it is hardly surprising that the Youth Service has virtually no contact with those young people who are in full-time higher education. It is in its present form a monument to the social and cultural chasm that exists between our young educational elite and the rest. The public funds channelled through the NUS for the social and cultural activities of students are given with virtually no strings attached; but for the majority, access to public funds depends upon them surrendering a measure of autonomy and accepting the preordained leadership of an externally appointed youth leader. This they appear increasingly unwilling to do. The Latey Committee found that their witnesses aged seventeen and over saw themselves as adults,[9] so that when 'youth club membership underlines non-adult status, dependence and exclusion from the real world' it is perhaps inevitable that young people 'allow themselves to suffer comparatively little from this indignity'.[10] The result is, as Kuenstler found from his study of spontaneous independent youth groups, that those young people who form them are those 'with particular initiative, with self-confidence and energy and an eager desire to achieve their own failures and successes . . . who find no scope to exercise their powers or imagined powers within their organisations.'[11]

If the Youth Service in no way confers upon its clients adult status then young people are as Kuenstler found obliged to seek it elsewhere via alternative routes. To quote Abrams and Little:[12]

> There are two possibilities for the young to assert their identity in a society like Britain; they may rebel overtly against the old – in the manner of the Mods and Rockers or the New Left; or they may rebel against the status of youth itself – against the roles imposed as proper for one 'at that age' by the old. The former is the most conspicuous rebellion, but the latter is the more effective. What is involved in the latter, however, is very largely a determination to behave as, and be treated as, an adult. Early marriage, not Beatlemania, is the real act of defiance, the real escape from the social 'place' the old would like one to occupy. And the majority of the young resolve the ambiguities of their position in this way and not by any effort to be conspicuously youthful. The audience for pop music is fast becoming a child audience. A distinctive politics of youth has as little to recommend it to most young people as any other course of action that is distinctively of their age group.

Therein lies the nub of the argument, the reason why all purely 'youth' interventions founder, why the Youth Service has been singularly lacking in impact, why both national and local government agencies deem it to be marginal and even at times to be dispensable, why central government has lacked even the interest to formulate a coherent 'youth policy' of its own. As the following news item clearly shows, the Government at the present juncture sees the Youth Service as collectively having little worthwhile to contribute to even the most general educational discussion.[13]

Attempts by the National Association of Youth Clubs to take part in the National Education Debate have been rebuffed by the DES. NAYC approached the Minister of Education, Shirley Williams, with a request to be allowed to take part but were told that it was not possible to include every organisation with 'some such interest'.

The DES has shown itself to be quite content to delegate its responsibility regarding the Youth Service to the LEAs although it cannot but be aware that in many areas 'this means that bad will become worse',[14] or that in the absence of firm direction that the LEAs will ensure that financial exigencies will 'strike first at adult education and youth work provision'.[15] Faced with this widespread indifference to the needs of the Youth Service in many quarters those responsible for the day-to-day administration of youth work provision still tend to react in a predictable fashion, arguing that failure to support the Youth Service financially will open the floodgates of delinquency. Such pleas may have worked in the days prior to Albemarle, before in fact the experiment had been tried and found wanting, but sixteen years later such dire warnings appear to have only minimal impact, for few believe that 'Unless, the Youth and Community Service, along with other non-mandatory local services, is afforded a minimum of protection against financial cutbacks, social disquiet from the younger generation will rapidly escalate beyond levels experienced hitherto.'[16]

The Youth Service has not in the past and does not appear likely in the future to be capable of offering a coherent policy or programme with regard to such areas of concern as delinquency, vandalism, youth unemployment, teenage alcohol abuse or truancy. It is powerless to influence the root causes, so unfortunately it can rarely effect a cure. When the 'youth problem' scarcely amounted to more than keeping them 'off the streets', as during the 1939–45 period, then the Youth Service was able to claim a measure of success. In the late 1970s when the problems are overwhelmingly symptomatic of far more intractable structural problems emanating from long-term industrial decline, urban deprivation and widespread alienation, then the Youth Service is quite simply not up to the task. In fact, the drift towards school-based provision may well as Booton suggests be making it increasingly unable to even contribute to the collective effort to solve these problems.[17]

The immediate future seems depressing. By the end of the present year we shall have close on three quarters of a million unemployed young people. The school-based sector is currently doing virtually no work with unemployed youth. The number of indictable offences committed by the juvenile and adolescent age groups will probably reach another all-time record, and over 70% of those kids will be in the school age range. Apart from one or two I.T. schemes, the school sector of Youth Service has yet to record any significant achievements in preventative work.

Even those with titular responsibility for the maintenance of the Youth Service have begun to openly question its long-term worth. As one Director of Education put it: 'Indeed, I will go so far as to say that the Youth Service as such has outworn its usefulness and ought to be allowed to wither away quietly.'[18] Such opinions understandably are rarely verbalized, but policy decisions at both a macro and micro level lend considerable credibility to the view that they are not restricted solely to those who publicly proclaim them. Certainly neither central nor local government can be absolved from blame if the Youth Service is once again 'withering away'. Whatever the causes, such a decline however, raises yet again the question of whether public funds should be made available in an attempt to reverse the trend of the last decade. Even if sufficient funds were to be made available, which is unlikely given the current economic and political climate, there seems little educational or social justification for rescuing organizations that appear progressively more and more incapable of attracting members aged fourteen and over. It appears unlikely that increased grant-aid will reverse trends that have been marked for at least twenty-five years, the voluntary organizations it seems must be left to find their own solutions to these problems or face a future that will entail catering for either an ever younger or diminishing clientele, or both.

For the statutory sector, the policy decisions are far more complex. Elements of this sector might well lend themselves to reform, for as Simpson has noted:[19]

Youth work has always included some of the essential features of community development. From the beginning of the century it placed emphasis upon helping groups of young people to become more precisely aware of their leisure needs, and to acquire and adapt their own premises and their own affairs with an eye to the needs of others in their neighbourhood. The idea of concern for the community as a whole is no new thing . . . but . . . it would however be misleading to suggest that activities along these lines formed more than a part of the youth scene. The larger part has been made up of recreative leisure pursuits and sociability. Indeed for a time, particularly when, immediately after the Albemarle Report, there was a generous provision of purpose-built clubs, centres, wings and leisure facilities, the features of youth work which are akin to community development tended to be overshadowed.

The likelihood of self-induced reforms taking place on a general scale seem to be slight, for as the average age of the membership has fallen so the concentration of resources upon the provision of leisure activities seems to have grown, and those young people who have an interest in community work have tended to affiliate to such groups as Shelter and the Neighbourhood Projects. The ethos of these groups is largely at variance with the concept of community work or service that is propounded by the Duke of Edinburgh Award Scheme and the uniformed organizations, and affiliation tends in no way to imply a loss of adult status.

A suggestion that is often discussed for reviving the fortunes of the Youth Service has been the proposal that the Government set up a Ministry of Youth or Youth Affairs. In its most sophisticated form it is envisaged that the national advisory body would be replicated at a local level, entailing the appointment of a high-ranking official whose brief would include the responsibility of evaluating all policy decisions to ensure that the 'special' needs of youth were fully recognized and taken cognizance of.[20] The idea is administratively inept and it is difficult to envisage how such individuals might operate in practise. Also and perhaps the pre-eminent objection, is that there appears to be no overriding justification for the creation of a Minister of Youth any more than there is for the appointment of a Minister of Children, OAPs, Women, or any other demographic group.

The idea would certainly not take us one step closer towards an acknowledgement of the fact that few young people require or demand access to separate provision; they rarely use that which is now provided and no evidence has yet been presented that would indicate that they would greet the initiatives of a Minister of Youth with any more fervour than they currently do those emanating from the LEA Youth Officers.

The problems of unemployment, poverty and homelessness certainly affect young people, but not simply in the one-dimensional form that the Youth Service usually discusses them. Parental unemployment creates serious difficulties for many school-age adolescents, poverty, homelessness and deprivation are all more likely to manifest themselves in a family context than outside it. In the case of unemployment it is certainly arguable that special policies and governmental initiatives relating to youth unemployment have been divisive and damaging to those young people who are still at school and whose parents are either unemployed or under-employed. As one study stressed:[21]

Being brought up in poverty, in a home where no one works, is likely to have more damaging effects on young people than a short spell of personal unemployment in young adulthood. Where public policy choices have to be made shouldn't we focus on the heads of households who have dependents?

There are few if any unique 'youth problems' and even fewer 'youth solutions', so that most attempts to find such solutions are futile and capable of producing only short-term answers at the best. They may satisfy the special pleadings of Youth Service administrators who retain a belief in the 'uniqueness' of the adolescent experience and the extent to which youth and their 'problems' can be isolated from the rest of society, but they are unlikely to satisfy anyone else, particularly the adolescents for whom they are designed.[22]

Much youth work is engaged upon the task of postponing maturity and extending the time-scale of adolescence. In the process it ties up a great deal of plant, personnel and resources that might be more effectively transferred to the support of community social provision that strives to eliminate divisions based upon age rather than giving them added form. Social Services can be left, given adequate resources, to deal with the special needs of young people 'at risk'; schools can be entrusted to cater for the education of children, and wherever possible the community including young people can be left free to determine, if given the resources, their own leisure patterns. The majority of young persons already do this, they are unattached or in such irregular contact with the Youth Service that they might for all practical purposes be placed in that category, and no research has yet shown that they are in any way worse off, deprived or under-privileged, for that absence of contact. As Mays found in his Liverpool survey carried out over twenty years ago: 'If young people are genuinely interested in the pursuits of an activity, they may be relied upon to provide their own dynamism and leadership.'[23] It is perhaps time that this was recognized and resources allocated accordingly, for the truth of the matter is that after a plethora of reports and discussion papers: 'We simply do not know what the community wants; either what young people want for themselves or what others want for them.'[24]

Notes

Preface

1 F. Parkin (1970), p.145.
2 G. Aves (1969), p.95, is only able to quote one other public agency that has for 'many years . . . directly recruited and organised voluntary workers', in any significant numbers.
3 R. Crossman (1973) *The Times*, 8 August 1973.
4 J. Ewen (1975), p.19.
5 G. Aves (1969).

Chapter 1   The early years

1 The 'rescue' function of early youth work, epitomized in the work of such individuals as Quintin Hogg in Charing Cross, Charles Baker in Bayswater, General Gordon in Gravesend and countless others whose efforts go unrecorded, concentrated upon helping those young people, usually the most underprivileged, who were not catered for by other agencies. As the Rev. E. Clark, who founded a club in Dover in 1858 explained, his club was designed to cater for 'Boys of 14 to 19, too young for membership of Mechanics' Institutes, too well-dressed for Ragged Night Schools, too proud for Free Schools, too indolent or too tired to apply themselves to the teaching given in schools of a higher sort'. Quoted in W.M. Eager (1953), p.158.
2 There is simply no adequate, let alone definitive, history of the Youth Service. Histories exist of the individual organizations, W.M. Eager (1953) and F. Dawes (1975) on the Boys' Club Movement; O. Coburn (1950) on the YHA Movement; A.E. Birch (1959) on the Boys' Brigade and E.E. Reynolds (1950) on the Scout Movement. Only A. Percival (1951) presents a more general history.
3 1872 saw the first recorded use of the title 'club'. Established by the Rev. D. Elsdale in Camberwell, the 'club' opened three nights per week to cater for the leisure needs of boys and youths.
4 J. Scott Lidgett quoted by F. Milson (1970), p.41.
5 A. Devine (1891), quoted by W.M. Eager (1953), p.269.
6 T.W.H. Pelham (1888), quoted by B. Simon (1965), p.70.
7 See F. Dawes (1975) and W.M. Eager (1953).
8 See P.H.J.H. Gosden (1973) for a comprehensive history of these endeavours; also J. Foster (1974) for a more detailed examination of their development in one small industrial town.

9   J. Burns (1889) in R. Frow, E. Frow and M. Katanka (eds) (1971), p.115.
10 J. Macalister Brew (1957), p.119.
11 W. Ashworth (1960), p.140.
12 R.C.K. Ensor (1936), p.109.
13 H. Perkin, (1969), pp.426–7 stresses that by the end of the nineteenth century 'with industrial opportunities declining on the one side and educational opportunities disappearing on the other, upward mobility for the working class was probably at its nadir'.
14 R. Pinker (1971), p.68.
15 H. Perkin (1969), p.258.
16 E.J. Hobsbawm (1969), p.238. Dicey defined collectivism as 'that which favours the intervention of the State, even at some sacrifice of individual freedom, for the purpose of conferring benefit upon the mass of the people' (1914), p.64.
17 D. Fraser (1973), p.129.
18 A.J. Balfour (1895) quoted in E. Halevy (1951), p.231.
19 R.M. Titmuss (1974), p.80.
20 HMSO (1904), p.96.
21 E.J. Hobsbawm (1969), p.165.
22 H. Perkin (1969), p.448.
23 O. Hill (1889) quoted by W.M. Eager (1953), p.316. Eager (p.315) comments that the Army Cadet Force failed to attract middle-class boys and consequently did not seriously develop until the 1880s when it was sponsored by individuals such as Octavia Hill and F.F. Vane 'who were concerned for working boys'. In 1886 after a lengthy debate and despite opposition from its Liberal supporters Toynbee Hall sponsored a unit of the Army Cadet Force.
24 The main uniformed youth groups in order of appearance were: The Army Cadet Force (1860); the Boys' Brigade (1883); the Church Lads' Brigade (1891); the Sea Cadet Force (1895); the Girls' Life Brigade (1902); the Boy Scouts (1907) and the Girl Guides (1910).
25 T. Arnold quoted S.J. Curtis and M.E.A. Boultwood (1960), p.112.
26 Smith was a Non-Conformist so the Boys' Brigade with its close attachment to that faith largely recruited boys sympathetic to the Free Churches. The Brigade's immense popularity however prompted men of different religious persuasions to establish groups closely modelled on the ideas of Smith; these were 'The Church Lads' (Anglican – 1891), 'The Roman Catholic Boys' Brigade' (1900), and the 'Jewish Lads' Brigade' (1895).
27 W. Smith (1889) quoted in B. Davies and A. Gibson (1967), p.42.
28 Quoted in F. Dawes (1975), p.62.
29 W. Smith quoted in F.P. Gibbon (1934), p.78.
30 W. Smith (1899) quoted in F.P. Gibbon (1934), p.125. For a contemporary reiteration of this view see D.J. Wilson-Haffenden, (1967), p.237–9.
31 George VI (1943) quoted A.E. Birch (1965), p.71.
32 'Aids to Scouting' was a manual prepared by Baden-Powell for

training boy soldiers; it was adopted apparently much to his surprise by Boys' Brigade companies and schools for teaching purposes. Smith asked him to re-write the book for working with civilian boys. This he did and it was published as 'Scouting for Boys'.

33 The relationship between the two organizations during the early years of Scouting is discussed in H. Collis *et al.* (1961), pp.48-9 and A.E. Birch (1965), pp.40-3.
34 R. Baden-Powell (1937), p.13.
35 R. Baden-Powell (1937), p.319.
36 The uniform, for example, 'was taken from a sketch of my own dress in Kashmir, 1897, in every detail, including belt, hat, staff, shirt, shorts, neckerchief, knife, rolled coat, etc.' Baden-Powell quoted by A.C. Percival (1951), p.119.
37 Boy Scout Association (1910) quoted by E.E. Reynolds (1950), p.1.
38 L. Elvin (1969), p.88.
39 F. Dawes (1975), p.61.
40 For a full discussion of this see P. Freire (1972), pp.45-59.
41 For a full breakdown of the membership figures of the Boy Scouts from 1908 onwards see H. Collis *et al.* (1959), pp.257-308.
42 R. Baden-Powell (1929), p.7.
43 Scouting was outlawed in Stalinist Russia, Nazi Germany and Fascist Italy during the inter-war years and in their client states. Significantly the rise of Fascism led to the Fourth Scout Law being amended in 1934 to read 'A Scout is a friend to all and a brother to every other Scout, no matter to what country, class or creed the other may belong'.
44 C.E.B. Russell (1932), p.15.
45 W.M. Eager (1953), p.342.
46 C.E.B. Russell (1932), p.31.
47 F. Dawes (1975), pp.100-1.
48 Eager reports that as early as 1870 certain clubs in Lancashire were already so obsessed with achieving sporting success that they were employing professional players to strengthen their football teams.
49 F. Dawes (1975), p.101.
50 W.M. Eager (1953), p.343.
51 L. Paul (1950), p.51.
52 A. Marwick (1965), p.125.
53 This figure according to Marwick does not include 'the countless other children set to work in total violation of the law', p.125.
54 C. Leeson (1917), p.9. Leeson as a leading member of the Howard Association might have been expected to have chosen his words more carefully, for on average crime during the war period only exceeded the 1912 figures for both Indictable and Non-Indictable Offences in one year, 1917. In fact with regard to Non-Indictable Offences, 1916 provided the lowest figures for any year during the period spanning 1893 to 1965. In reality the 'crime-wave' nationally amounted to only 701 additional juvenile offenders being charged

between December 1914 and December 1915 (figures quoted by Leeson, p.15). In the City of Liverpool the 'plague' represented 24 additional convictions. For complete data on conviction rates for the war years see B.R. Mitchell and H. Jones (1971), p.204.

55 Board of Education Report (1917), Cmnd 9045.

56 Quoted in report of National Council of Public Morals (1917), pp.204–5.

57 Cmnd 8512.

58 W. Ashworth (1960), pp.301–2.

59 A.S. Milward (1970), p.23. See also P. Abrams (1963) on the social reforms proposed by the Ministry of Reconstruction.

60 It was envisaged that the day continuation schools would offer part-time compulsory education for those aged 14 to 16 who were no longer in full-time education or attending day courses at technical or art colleges. A few were set up by individual employers in co-operation with LEAs, but by 1937 only Rugby had introduced a compulsory universal LEA scheme which was catering for 1200 adolescents. Nationally the picture sixteen years after Geddes was bleak; out of a total of 2,531,000 young people eligible, 20,550 were attending either Rugby or one of the privately funded schools and 106,526 were enroled on college courses; this meant that only 5 per cent were being catered for. See A.E. Morgan (1939), pp.15–21.

61 Final Report of the Adult Education Committee of the Ministry of Reconstruction. Cmnd 321. (1919).

62 W.M. Evans (1965), p.13.

63 D. Hawes (1966), p.50.

64 A.E. Morgan (1939), p.374

65 This 'hostility' towards alternative forms of provision is reflected in the attitude of a leading member of the NABC (National Association of Boys' Clubs) who writes that following the initiations of the "immediate post-war period they became 'a species of "Juvenile Organisation", classified not only with Brigades and Scouts, but with long-haired enthusiasms, labelled with high-fautin' names, of which the friendly, sporting, sensible and humorous working boy would fight shy. Fads, Fancies and Fanaticisms – this queer feminism which would affiliate Boys' Clubs to Girls' Club Federations.' W.M. Eager (1953), pp.410–11.

66 For a full account of the life and work of Henry Morris and his contribution to community education see H. Reé (1973).

67 C. Cameron, A. Lush and G. Meara (1943), p.121.

68 A.E. Morgan (1939), p.377. The Slough centre was according to Morgan, 'the largest and most expensive Community Centre built by a local authority'. It cost £18,000 of which half was borne by the Housing Committee and half by the Education Committee.

69 T.H. Marshall (1975), p.81.

70 See W. Hannington (1977) for an account of the NUWM opposition to the NCSS centres. See p.273–4.

71 D. Hanson (1972), p.636.

72 D. Hanson (1972), p.637, illustrates this point in his description of the 'model' NCSS centre at Butterknowle, Co. Durham. The centre set up to help unemployed miners had an NCSS appointed committee comprising 'the local vicar, the doctor, the postmaster, the head-teacher, two colliery owners, the chairman of the Parish Council and a solitary miner.'

73 C. Cameron *et al.* (1943), p.111.

74 C. Cameron *et al.* (1943), p.112 quote a full-time NCSS warden in Liverpool on this topic, 'Club organisation was . . . essentially undemocratic. It seems to have been based on the theory that unemployed men were unfitted to take any responsibility for their own Clubs and that Management Committees, by definition knew what was good for the men better than the men knew it themselves.'

75 See C. Cameron *et al.* (1943), p.111.

76 See V.A. Bell (1934) for a detailed history of the Juvenile Instruction Centres prior to 1933, pp.1–25.

77 R. Pope (1977), p.28.

78 E. Salter-Davies (1933) estimated that only 24.7 per cent of unemployed boys and 17 per cent of unemployed girls were attending classes or centres in 1932. In Lancashire Pope put the percentage at 15 per cent for boys and girls combined.

79 A.E. Morgan (1939), p.100.

80 R. Pope (1977), p.32.

81 Ministry of Labour Circular 19/60 (1930).

82 H. Durant (1938), p.207.

83 A.E. Morgan (1939), p.393.

84 H. Durant (1938), p.208.

85 M. Rooff (1935), p.98. P.H.K. Kuenstler (1953), p.13, notes that it was 'an interesting sign of the times and changing semantics that in 1935 a rather different distinction was made between "voluntary helpers (leisured)" and "voluntary workers (in posts)", all of whom were voluntary leaders of clubs that differently engaged during the day.'

86 F. Dawes (1975), p.148.

87 E. Macadam (1934), p.301.

88 F. Dawes (1975), p.127.

89 F. Dawes (1975), p.151.

90 See A.E. Morgan (1939), pp.278–366 for a full breakdown of membership totals for the major national voluntary youth organizations.

91 R. Graves and A. Hodge (1955), p.215.

92 HMSO (1944a), para. 321.

93 C. Cameron *et al.* (1943), p.118.

94 A.E. Morgan (1939), pp.278–366.

95 F. Milson (1970), p.7.

96 Quoted in B. Davies and A. Gibson (1967), p.42.

97 W.M. Eager (1934) quoted F. Dawes (1975), p.146.

98 R. Benewick (1972), p.231.

99 W.M. Eager (1953), pp.263–4.
100 In a number of national organizations this debate was not resolved amicably and groups of members left to form separate organizations that enforced stricter conditions for membership. Splits of this kind occurred in the Boy Scouts, the Girl Guides, the YMCA and the YWCA during the 1920s and 1930s.
101 F. Dawes (1975), p.146.
102 See A.M. Herbert (1939).
103 J. Stevenson (1977), p.123.
104 A similar scheme was set up for girls with the Women's Section of the British Legion making facilities available to the Ministry of Labour, however due to lack of support it failed within a matter of months.
105 Quoted in R. Graves and A. Hodge (1955), p.381.
106 This amounted to £400,000 and was administered by King George's Field Association.
107 D. Fraser (1973), p.166.
108 Quoted by W. Hannington (1977), p.272. The percentage accepted equalled 30.2 per cent. W.H. Evans (1965), p.15, reports that by 1935 the acceptance rate stood at 37.5 per cent.
109 J. Stevenson (1977), pp.42–3.
110 Principles and Aims of the Boys' Club Movement (1930) reprinted in C.E.B. Russell and L.M. Russell (1932), p.17.
111 See O. Coburn (1950) for the history of the early years of the YHA.
112 See R. Graves and A. Hodge (1955), pp.265–80.
113 A.E. Morgan (1939), pp.389–91.
114 A.E. Morgan (1939), p.389.
115 Hansard, vol. 353 (1938–39), p.976 (Mr K. Lindsey).
116 Board of Education Circular 1516 (1940).
117 Hansard, vol. 376 (1941–2), p.1031. Circular 1577 and compulsory registration were not without their opponents at both a local and national level. These saw in it overtones of the Hitler Youth and similar totalitarian groups, embodying an unwarrented infringement upon individual liberty. See J.M. Brew (1944), pp.68–9 and W.H. Evans (1965), p.22.
118 G. Ette (1949), p.37.
119 K. Lindsey (1975), *Times Educational Supplement,* 1 August 1975.
120 W.H. Evans (1965), pp.23–4. Much of this success according to Brew was founded upon the role of youth centres as restaurants designed to offer unemployed young people cheap hot meals. Many placed menus outside their premises and not surprisingly it became 'commonplace to say that the canteen is the heart of the club'. J.M. Brew (1944), p.49.
121 National Youth Advisory Council established in 1939 by the Board of Education.
122 HMSO (1943), para. 40.
123 HMSO (1944b), Section 41(b).
124 HMSO (1944a), para. 339.

125 HMSO (1944a), para. 366.
126 The only surviving course was the one attached to University College, Swansea.
127 L. Button (1969), p.1.
128 The four emergency courses for training youth leaders set up during the 1939–45 period also closed before the Fletcher Committee published their report.
129 F. Milson (1970), p.11.
130 Lord Aberdare (1947) Chairman's address to the NABC annual conference.
131 SCNVYO (1945) quoted in A.C. Percival (1951), p. 178.
132 J. Maud (1951), p.17 – Ashridge Conference Report – King George's Jubilee Trust.
133 J. Maud (1951), p.16 – Ashridge Conference Report – King George's Jubilee Trust.
134 Maud talked in terms of an attachment rate of between 40 per cent and 25 per cent; three years earlier Ward has estimated 77 per cent.
135 J. Longland (1951), p.45 – Ashridge Conference Report – King George's Jubilee Trust.
136 A King George VI Leadership Certificate was introduced for part-time youth leaders; it was however a lengthy and demanding course which attracted few students.
137 Ashridge Conference Report (1951), p.54.
138 E. Younghusband (1951), p.103.
139 P.H.K. Kuenstler (1953), p.16.
140 HMSO (1960a), para. 246.
141 O. Watkins (1972), p.5 and HMSO (1960), para. 246.
142 P.H.K. Kuenstler (1953), p.16.
143 HMSO (1960a), para. 287.
144 King George's Jubilee Trust (1955), p.109.
145 T.R. Fyvel (1961), p.253.
146 M. Thomas and J. Perry (1975), p.58.
147 HMSO (1960a), para. 1.

Chapter 2   The Albemarle years

1 J. Eggleston (1976), p.63. See also T.S. Chivers (1977), p.25, who endorses this finding.
2 HMSO (1956), Seventh Report – Select Committee on Estimates.
3 House of Lords, vol. 213 (8 December 1958 – 5 February 1959), pp.1052–1176.
4 King George's Jubilee Trust (1955).
5 B. Roshier (1973) in his survey of crime coverage as a percentage of total news space in the Daily Mirror, Daily Express, Daily Telegraph and News of the World for the period 1938–67 found that this peaked during the period 1950–55, thus the decline in official rates of crime (non-motoring) was in no way matched by a reduction in coverage, the reverse in fact taking place. Paradoxically after

1955 as the crime rate increased coverage declined, particularly in the News of the World, where by 1962 it had fallen to nearly a third of its 1955 level. See also S. Chibnall (1977), pp.46–7.

6   T.R. Fyvel (1961), p.14.

7   A campaign similar to that mounted by the Daily Mirror in the late 1950s was initiated by the Scottish Daily Express during 1968 and 1969, even down to a well publicized voluntary surrender of weapons. This particular campaign was centred upon teenage groups active in the Easterhouses area of Glasgow. The underlying political motivation for this campaign and the effect it had upon the community concerned are described in an article by G. Armstrong and M. Wilson (1973). S. Cohen (1972) also deals at length with the media's handling of the 'mods' and 'rockers' confrontation circa 1965, see pp.31–48.

8   L.L. Loewe (1976), p.76.

9   HMSO (1959), Cmnd. 1213. The 1961 Criminal Justice Act also dealt with custodial establishments for young offenders.

10 T.R. Fyvel (1961), p.64. See also Council of Europe (1960) for a discussion of the 'problem' in its wider European context.

11 M. Abrams (1959).

12 J. Coleman (1961) (see note no.16) and S.N. Eisenstadt (1956).

13 K. Keniston (1960).

14 J. Webb (1962), B. Jackson and D. Marsden (1962) also the earlier study of W. Waller (1932) carried out in the USA.

15 T. Parsons (1942), p.604. K. Davis (1940) in an earlier article adopts a similar stance to that of Parsons in maintaining that 'The much publicised critical attitude of youth towards established ways is partly a matter of being on the outside looking in'. p.529.

16 American studies of the 'youth problem' tend to pre-date their British and European counterparts, possibly because the American war boom of the 1940s was nearly a full decade before its European equivalent. See for example D.M. Potter (1954), 'People of Plenty'.

17 W. Watson (1962), pp.42–3.

18 J. Coleman (1961), p.3. D.C. Epperson (1964) criticizes Coleman's study on the grounds that his research shows that the indices adopted by Coleman grossly exaggerated the degree of adult-youth divergence.

19 M. Abrams (1959), p.10.

20 M. Abrams (1967), p.446. To curtail this expenditure it was seriously suggested in a bulletin to schools that 'a teenage tax could be introduced that would be of educational as well as economic value'. This was apparently widely debated as a realistic proposal, see F.L. Ralphs (1967), p.442.

21 Mark Abrams was in fact part author of 'Must Labour Lose?' (1960) with Richard Rose, a *locus classicus* of the embourgeoisement thesis.

22 See G. Murdock and R. McCron (1976), pp.10–26, for a fuller discussion of this point.

23 M. McLuhan (1970), p.142. See also C. Adelman (1973).
24 M. McLuhan (1970), p.27.
25 See C. Hamblett and J. Deverson (1964); G. Hechinger and
    G.M. Hechinger (1964); J. Nuttall (1968). According to S. Chibnall
    (1977) p.93, for the media 'Youth . . . had been the pre-eminent
    metaphor of social change in the post-war years'.
26 See the review of B. Davies (1976) of 'Resistance Through Rituals'
    and the response to it from D. Marsland and P. Hunter (1976), also
    J. Clark (1976), D. Smith (1976).
27 This was perhaps inevitable given the source of many of these
    writings. Emanating from certain sections of the New Left and
    followers of Marcuse, who accepted in part the 'embourgeoise-
    ment thesis', they saw young people and racial minorities in the
    advanced capitalist nations forming along with liberation move-
    ments in the Third World the new revolutionary vanguard; a van-
    guard untainted by the trappings of affluence. Unfortunately for a
    while after the events of May 1968 they all too often came to
    believe their own propaganda, making sometimes preposterous
    assumptions regarding the political content and significance of
    teenage culture; see in particular J. Rowntree and M. Rowntree
    (1968), also D. Widgery (1976), pp.306–40; H. Marcuse (1969);
    E. Mandel (1970); D. Cohn-Bendit (1969); and F. Halliday (1969).
    Two British groups, the SLL (Socialist Labour League, later to
    become the Workers' Revolutionary Party) and the RSL (Revolu-
    tionary Socialist League), better known as the 'Militant Group',
    from 1960 onwards orientated themselves, almost to the exclusion
    of everything else, to working amongst young people. The activities
    of the SLL eventually obliged the Labour Party to close down their
    Young Socialists for twelve months in 1964, while the RSL now
    virtually control the reformed Labour Party Young Socialists,
    which they manipulate as a semi-autonomous group within the
    parent party. For a full history of these developments see
    Z. Layton-Henry (1976), pp.290–308.
28 See in particular B. Davies (1969), F.W. Musgrove (1964),
    pp.84–105, and the National Children's Bureau (1976) report
    'Britain's Sixteen Year Olds'.
29 S. Cohen (1973), p.180.
30 J. Henry (1972), p.157.
31 Quoted in J.A. Hadfield (1962), p.280.
32 F.L. Ralphs (1967).
33 S. Cohen (1973), p.192. The reference to Bank Holidays alludes to
    the Mods and Rockers disturbances of 1965 and 1966.
34 See for example J.E. Meade (1964), R. Blackburn (1967) and
    R.J. Nicholson (1967).
35 For a detailed discussion of this process see M. Young and
    P. Willmott (1973), especially pp.19–22.
36 See for example N.J. Gibson (1966), pp.86–93 and J.M. Livingston
    (1966), pp.44–51.
37 A. Gamble and P. Walton (1976), p.1.

38   H. Watkinson speaking 22 January 1958. This theme was to be
     reiterated by Harold MacMillan (22 October 1959) who with due
     deference to the memory of Disraeli announced that 'Britain has
     ceased to be two nations'.
39   P.H. Partridge (1961) reprinted 1967 in A. Quinton (ed) (1967),
     p.37.
40   E.P. Thompson (1976), p.84.
41   N. Mailer (1957), p.291–3, interestingly in his discussion of the
     hipster-beatnik life-style, accepts this epithet, referring to the
     hipster 'as a new breed of adventurer . . . a philosophical psycho-
     path'.
42   S. Cohen (1973), p.56, in a survey found boredom and affluence as
     the most often quoted causes of delinquency. H. Swados (1958),
     p.224, talks 'of the tormenting discontent of an American youth
     for which everything is being done, to which everything is being
     given . . . except a reason for living and for building a socially
     useful life'.
43   S. Cohen (1973), p.89. In a survey of possible solutions to the
     'problem' of mods and rocker violence, Cohen found 81 per cent
     of respondents favoured 'Hard Solutions' – stiffer sentences, more
     discipline, tougher police powers, etc., only 19 per cent saw options
     such as strengthening home life, building up citizenship etc., as
     relevant.
44   HMSO (1960a), para. 75.
45   D. Hawes (1966), p.5.
46   E. Goffman (1959), p.20.
47   H. Eysenck (1969), p.688.
48   HMSO (1960a), p.13. This view endorsed that of the King George's
     Jubilee Trust (1955) working party which found that as far as
     National Service was concerned 'there is little that is fundamentally
     wrong with the present system . . . there can be no doubt that the
     majority benefit . . . from the point of view of physical fitness and
     character development', p.133.
49   King George's Jubilee Trust (1955) recommended that the break
     with home ties should be as complete as was practical for National
     Servicemen if it was to aid personal development. They recom-
     mended the restriction of weekend leave and that 'all National
     Servicemen should be sent abroad as soon as they are trained',
     pp.117–18.
50   D.F. Greenberg (1977), pp.189–223.
51   W.H. Evans (1965), p.76.
52   HMSO (1960a), p.1.
53   R. Hamilton (1972), p.17.
54   For a discussion of the relationship between the concept of terri-
     tory and 'teddy boy' gang violence see D. Downes (1966), p.119
     and T. Jefferson (1976), p.81.
55   T. Jefferson (1976), p.83, claims that the Notting Hill riot grew
     out of an incident involving nine 'Teds'.
56   See T.R. Fyvel (1963), p.119. Also J. Clarke *et al.* (1975).

57 T. Jefferson (1976), p.83.
58 For a graphic account of the political style and background of the
    Yippies see N. Mailer (1969), pp.83–216.
59 The impact of 'political' pop was it appears mainly upon middle-
    class adolescents. G. Murdock and G. Phelps (1972) found that the
    often more political pop of adult-disapproved performers 'particu-
    larly attracted the interest of grammar school school-rejectors'
    (p.48) who tended to be far more involved in 'pop culture' than
    either secondary school pupils or their fellow grammar school
    pupils. Similar research carried out in the USA by J.P. Robinson
    and P.M. Hirsh quoted by Murdock and Phelps found 'that high-
    school pupils from middle class homes were more than twice as
    likely as pupils from working class homes to list "protest" songs as
    their favourites, i.e. records with lyrics which served to articulate
    oppositional values. Working-class pupils, on the other hand, were
    very much more likely to nominate routine "Top Twenty" records
    which contained no oppositional content'.
60 I.L. Horowitz and M. Liebowitz (1968), p.285.
61 For an account of this 'merger' see G. Pearson (1975), pp.79–120.
    N. Fountain (1968) offers an amusing account of one particularly
    crude attempt to marry the politics of the New Left to the 'pop
    scene' which illustrates clearly the gulf that existed between the
    two.
62 HMSO (1960a), para. 68.
63 HMSO (1960a), para. 69.
64 HMSO (1960a), para. 69.
65 This lack of research allowed the prejudices of the panel free rein.
    Throughout it defines juvenile crime as a working class phenom-
    enon. Later research, admittedly American in origin, seriously
    questions such an assumption. H.L. Voss (1966), Erickson and
    Empey (1965) and more recently, D.E. Frease (1972–3) and C.R.
    Tittle and W.J. Villemez (1977). All imply that the relationship
    between crime and class amongst juveniles is very problematic, but
    it is largely a *pro rata* one relating to the numerical size of the
    social classes. Applied to Britain, working-class delinquents would
    predominate simply because they were members of the largest
    class.
66 By 1971, theft and unauthorised taking amounted to 33,000 indict-
    able offences among young persons aged 17 and under, while the
    total of 27,000 cases brought under the Highway Act was second,
    these two combined with Burglary and Robbery provided over
    80 per cent of all convictions.
67 J. Young (1970).
68 For a discussion of the role of the press as amplifiers of deviancy
    during the 1950s see S. Chibnall (1977), pp.46–74.
69 F.K. Heussenstamm (1971), pp.27–31. In the study referred to
    fifteen drivers with no previous traffic violations for the preceding
    twelve months attached Black Panther stickers to their bumpers
    and acquired thirty-three citations in seventeen days.

70   R.A. Scott (1972), p.29.
71   HMSO (1960a), para. 65.
72   HMSO (1960a), para. 3.
73   F.W. Musgrove (1964), p.154.
74   W.H. Evans (1965), p.154.
75   Derbyshire Education Authority (1967), p.8.
76   D. Hawes (1966), p.5.
77   For a fuller discussion of the long-term implications to the Youth Service of this failure to acquire a specific legislative structure see J. Parr (1972).

Chapter 3   Thinking it out

1   See W.H. Evans (1965), p.65, also T.S. Chivers (1977), p.7.
2   HMI Report, Ministry of Education (1966).
3   For a complete breakdown of comparative rates of LEA expenditure on youth provision see HMSO (1960), appendix 4, pp.119–27.
4   In 1957–8, 95 LEAs employed no full-time youth workers in any capacity at all, a further 41 maintained no local authority centres or youth wings. Source HMSO (1960), appendix 4, pp.114–27.
5   Ministry of Education Building Bulletin no.20 (1961). Withywood was also the subject of a widely shown film produced by the University of Bristol.
6   P. Ackroyd (1970), p.32.
7   F. Dawes (1975), p.180.
8   Quoted by T.H. Bristow (1970), p.22. See also R. Larkin (1972), pp.9–10, 'Youth Club or Palais?', for an analysis of the reasons given by young people aged seventeen to twenty for their preference for commercial provision as opposed to that offered by the Youth Service.
9   HMSO (1969), para. 16.
10   D.E. Ince (1971), p.46.
11   HMSO (1969), para. 2.
12   F. Dawes (1975), p.180, describes how the Withywood design 'sent a shiver down the spines of old boys' club men' when it was opened in 1961.
13   HMSO (1960a), para. 366.
14   The National College was initially a semi-autonomous agency financed directly by the Ministry of Education and managed by a Governing Body appointed by the Minister. In 1971 it ceased operating as a separate institution and the bulk of the staff were transferred to the City of Leicester College of Education where a new two year Youth and Community Training Course was initiated. In 1976 the City of Leicester College was merged with Leicester Polytechnic who now run the two year course. For a history of the National College (1961–70) see O. Watkins (1972).
15   J. Parr (1969), figures presented in Appendix 7 of his study.
16   By 1969 30 per cent of the 1961 intake of students were still employed full-time in youth and community work and 36.9 per

cent of the 1962 intake held senior management posts. 73 per cent
of the students who attended the National College between 1961
and 1970 who were in the youth and community sector were
employed by LEAs. Source: O. Watkins (1972), pp.108-25.

17 J. Ewen (1972), p.6.
18 J. Roth (1971), p.159.
19 One training course was described to its students as based on 'a
    model for the design of trainings based on the concept of initial
    and terminal behaviours, seeing the behavioural gap as the learning
    process'. (Youth Service Information Centre – Training Bulletin
    October 1971.) A description hardly likely to engender confidence
    amongst the uninitiated.
20 A. Dearling (1973), p.6.
21 T. Lovett (1973), p.23.
22 D.E. Ince (1971), p.14.
23 J. Ewen (1972), p.7.
24 J. Eggleston (1976), pp.143-4.
25 The National College had a minimum age of admission of 23 and
    an average student age of 28 to 30. O. Watkins (1972), p.12.
26 E. Hopper and M. Osborn (1975), p.94.
27 ibid. pp.94-5.
28 O. Watkins (1972), p.16. The decline in the percentage of students
    entering LEA youth work after completing their National College
    course was marked. In 1962 80 per cent obtained LEA posts, in
    1966 – 87 per cent. It then fell to 77 per cent in 1967, 70 per cent
    in 1968 and finally to 67 per cent in 1969. O. Watkins (1972),
    pp.108-9.
29 NAYSO (1974), reprinted National Youth Bureau (1975), vol.1.
30 V. Godby and P. Key (1975). The figures for the respective institu-
    tions were, Leicester – 23.5 per cent; Manchester – 9.4 per cent;
    Liverpool (NABC) – 14.1 per cent; Goldsmith's, London – 10.6 per
    cent; Westhill, Birmingham – 22.3 per cent; London (YMCA) –
    20.1 per cent.
31 H.A. Jones (1975), p.19.
32 J.T. Parr (1969), p.248. Regarding this point F. Milson (1970),
    p.98, compares the post-qualification experience of teachers and
    youth workers . He writes, 'At the end of three years the first go to
    their first school where they are junior members of staff, supported
    by more experienced colleagues. The second, after two years, may
    be in charge of a centre with several hundred members facing un-
    supported by professional colleagues, diverse demands.'
33 A youth worker in Newcastle reported that a youth and community
    post advertised in October 1977, (JNC scale II) attracted nine
    applications. Of these only one was from a trained youth and com-
    munity worker; seven were invited for interview, only two appeared,
    no explanation or apology was forthcoming from the five who
    failed to turn up. The two who did come were both unemployed
    teachers, one of whom was appointed. Before the closing date for
    applications a lecturer at a nearby institution involved in running a

full-time youth and community training course, was contacted and
he reported that none of his former students who were still unemployed were interested in even applying.
34 HMSO (1960a), para. 277.
35 HMSO (1960a), para. 258.
36 HMSO (1960a), para. 258.
37 L. Button (1969), p.2.
38 M. Clemans (1966), p.11. J. Eggleston (1976), p.23, estimates that
these courses had in 1975 750 students on them, giving an annual
output of approximately 250. The drastic reduction in the number
of trainee teachers is reducing this number yearly.
39 L. Button (1969), p.19. This total does not include four ex-students
who were full-time youth workers for less than two years, before
they found alternative employment.
40 The instances of job scarcity for the two-year trained worker are
often localized as is the prevalence of teacher recruitment. Perhaps
the most notable example of this is in Leicestershire where students
for the Leicester Polytechnic youth and community course are
often recruited from the immediate locality. They are however unable to obtain employment in their own LEA area as youth workers
due to a teacher only policy.
41 T.S. Chivers (1977), p.14.
42 T.S. Chivers (1977), p.10.
43 T.S. Chivers (1977), p.13.
44 T.J. Parr (1969). Parr graphically shows the wide variations in the
degree of professional mobility that exist within different sectors
of the Youth Service. Amongst LEA workers 57.7 per cent had
been in youth work for 3 years or less and a mere 10 per cent had
10 or more years full-time experience. Amongst YMCA/YWCA
leaders, who Parr estimates comprise 13 per cent of all full-time
youth workers, only 16.6 per cent had less than 3 years under their
belts, 26.6 per cent had between 7 and 9 years, 29.4 per cent
between 10 and 24 years and an impressive 16.6 per cent had over
30 years.
45 R. Fisher (1975), p.11. This is confirmed by the recently published
figures for January 1976 to July 1977. These show that '348 people
holding teaching qualifications entered full-time youth and community work. This represents 56 per cent of total entrants and
compares with 117 (19 per cent) entering from the specialist
training agencies, which give youth and community work qualifications' – 'Youth Work – Scene' no.31, March 1978.
46 See for example W.A. Teale (Principal Youth Officer for Lincoln-
shire) (1974), also D. Marsland and M. Day (1975), who collectively
advocate an all-graduate youth work profession. A theme that is
taken up by the Carnegie Working Party Report (1977) which urges
all graduate entry for the Scottish Youth and Community Service
'at the earliest possible date'. The case for all graduate entry has
been strenuously opposed by J. Ewen (late Director of the National
Youth Bureau) (1975), A. Oxford (1975) and R. Hamilton (1972).

The debate continues unabated, but in the light of the Carnegie Report it could be argued that the likelihood of an all-graduate profession in the near future cannot be discounted.

47 M. Barnsley (1972), p.20.
48 H. Haywood (1971), p.7.
49 See National Youth Bureau (1975).
50 These include courses established at Bulmershe College of Higher Education, North Wales Institute of Higher Education (Wrexham), Crewe and Alsager College of Higher Education, University of Durham, Ilkley College, Matlock College of Education and Sunderland Polytechnic.
51 J. Ewen (1975), p.19.
52 HMSO (1960a), para. 288.
53 HMSO (1960a).
54 HMSO (1966).
55 J. Ewen (1975), p.10.
56 D. Hawes (1966), pp. 47–8, mentions in this context the independent training schemes operated by the Church of England Youth Council, the Association for Jewish Youth, and Methodist Association of Youth Clubs, the NABC and the YMCA and YWCA.
57 After local government reorganization in 1974, 19 LEAs had full-time training officers, the remainder had senior organizers who carried out this work in conjunction with other duties.
58 Quoted by F. Milson (1970), p.90.
59 D. Staton (Youth Officer, Darlington) (1971), pp.3–4. YSIC Training Bulletin, 15 October 1971.
60 J.C. Anderson (1975), p.4, in a survey of 'Bessey Type' courses organized by LEAs in Scotland found that only 21 per cent of participants were drawn from uniformed groups, 4 per cent from the YMCA, YWCA and church-based groups such as the Youth Fellowship and the remainder all came from LEA groups and clubs.
61 M. Day (1973), reviewing the Basic Training of LEAs in the Home Counties, highlighted the way in which the LEAs used the courses as not only a means of socializing the students into their style of working, but as way of recruiting part-time staff.
62 F. Milson (1970), p.91.
63 L.J. Barnes (1948), p.120.
64 T.S. Chivers (1977), p.7.
65 For an exposition of this opposition to direct LEA provision see K. Lindsay (1975), who advocates an overwhelmingly subsidiary role for them on the grounds that although 'it is expedient for local authorities to finance other bodies, independent and voluntary, to carry out projects and experiments, where initiatives and innovations are required, such experiments are more efficient, more democratic and above all much cheaper than the equivalent services run from the town hall'. *Times Educational Supplement*, 1 August 1975.
66 HMSO (1969). The Scottish Education Department Standing Consultative Council on Youth and Community Service published a remarkably similar document 'Community of Interests' (HMSO,

1968) whose recommendations pp.58–9 largely coincided with
those of the subsequent Fairbairn-Milson Report.
67   HMSO (1969), para. 164.
68   Calouste Gulbenkian (1968), p.22.
69   An idea of the political philosophy underpinning the Report can
be gleaned from later articles written by Fred Milson which called
for a fundamental change in youth work praxis that would see it
offering 'an invitation to young people to become involved in the
struggle to build a society that is just, compassionate and participant'. (*Times Educational Supplement*, 12 March 1971.)
70   Quoted by J. Eggleston (1976), p.23.
71   The Young Volunteer Force Foundation (YVFF) which was to an
extent a derivation of the US Peace Corps was set up in 1967 under
a Trust Deed sponsored by leading political figures drawn from all
the major parties. It was given for its first three years £1,000,000
by the DES; this was not renewed but private and business sponsors
as well as sympathetic local authorities helped to finance a limited
number of projects until in 1974 the Home Office under its Urban
Aid Programme revitalized the YVFF by funding twenty-two of
the remaining field projects plus contributing to the costs of its
HQ.
72   See in particular the comments of Sir R. Goodwin (1973).
73   F. Dawes (1975), pp.184–5.
74   M. Thatcher 29 March 1971. Hansard (Written Answers) vol. 814
pp.297–8.
75   F. Dawes (1975), p.185.
76   F. Milson (1971), *Times Educational Supplement*, 12 March 1971.
77   M. Thatcher, Hansard (Written Answers) vol. 814, p.298.
78   D. Howell quoted *Times Educational Supplement*, 2 April 1971.
79   Leicester Mercury 14 January 1970. F. Milson (1971b), also
reports the speech of a Councillor who advocated the trimming of
the Youth Service budget in his area on the grounds that there
should be 'no money for fun'.
80   See 'Education', 7 September 1976. 'Digest of LEA Provision'.
81   Hansard, 5 February 1975. Written Answers vol. 885, p.526.
82   DES (1975) reprinted in full in *Youth Service*, Autumn 1975.
83   J. Ewen (1975), p.26.
84   DES (1975), p.2.
85   National Youth Bureau.
86   These memoranda are published in *Youth Service*, Autumn 1975.
87   Community Relations Commission (1976), p.1.
88   Ibid.

Chapter 4   An uneasy marriage: schools and the Youth Service

1   F. Booton (1976), p.7.
2   R. Hamilton (1972), p.18.
3   F. Booton (1976), p.5. By 1976 all LEAs except one used schools
for youth activities and 66 out of 86 had opened purpose built

youth wings attached to secondary schools. Source: *Education* (1976), p.1.
4 F. Booton (1976), p.7. In 1975 the *Times Educational Supplement* carried 893 advertisements for full-time (non-officer) posts of which 338 (38 per cent) were school-based.
5 HMSO (1963), para. 24.
6 HMSO (1963), para. 136.
7 B. Russell (1916), p.100.
8 B. Russell (1938), p.305.
9 See G.H. Bantock (1975), pp.17–20. Bantock discusses the difficulties created for the school which adopts this alternative criterion and forcefully argues against the curriculum it can engender.
10 See for example A. Rowe (1971), pp.58–68, who deals with what he terms 'pointers to the kinds of success that can be measured' and specifically uses as his first 'pointer' the level of voluntary staying-on that a school achieves. It is a criterion under-written by the simple belief that 'more education is a "good" irrespective of whether or not a pupil gains examination qualifications'; as such it can be accused of confusing schooling with education, when obviously the two need not be synonymous, see P. Freire (1972).
11 Between 1965 and 1973 the percentage of pupils remaining at school after the age of 15 rose from 40.2 per cent to 58.6 per cent. Statistics of Education, vol.1. HMSO (1976), p.21.
12 DES announced that 83 per cent of school leavers in 1977 passed at least one public examination – *Guardian*, 7 April 1977.
13 HMSO (1974), pp.10–12.
14 R. Collins (1971), p.1007.
15 See S.A. Levitan and R. Taggart (1971). C. Jencks *et al.* (1972), p.87, referring to the extension of the period of schooling at the lower end of the statutory age range concluded that 'we cannot expect universal pre-schooling to narrow the gap between rich and poor or between whites and blacks. Universal pre-schooling might even widen the gap'. G. Smith and T. Jones (1975), in a British context arrived at a similar conclusion. Still, pound for pound, it would probably have been a better investment than ROSLA.
16 F. Parkin (1973), p.59.
17 For a discussion of this point see J. Westergaard and H. Resler (1975), in particular pp.319–42; J.H. Goldthorpe and P. Bevan (1977); A. Stanworth and A. Giddens (eds) (1974), pp.65–101; essays by R. Whitley and the editors.
18 How much of the much vaunted 'ROSLA money' actually filtered through to those for whom it was originally ear-marked is a moot point. ROSLA entitled one school in Leicestershire to a new general teaching block. When this was completed it became the Sixth Form Wing, while the old, by now ill-used and battered Sixth Form Block became the ROSLA base for the less academic Fifth Form groups. One suspects this was not an unusual occurrence. It certainly did not meet with any opposition from either the LEA or the teaching staff of the school. All were apparently

happy to see the academic hierarchy replicated in terms of physical provision.

19 See E. Bryne (1975), p.188, who quotes figures from one ROSLA 'interest based' group of courses in a 'Northern urban mixed Modern school which exported 88 per cent of girls leaving to unskilled or temporary jobs, 2 per cent of girls to further education, but 66 per cent of boys to skilled apprenticeships and 12 per cent to further education.'

20 Labour Party Policy Document (1973).

21 See S.A. Levitan and R. Taggart (1971), pp.97–135 and Y. Hasenfield (1975), pp.569–87, for a full discussion of employment needs of disadvantaged young people.

22 P. Wilby (1977), p.358. *New Statesman,* 17 September 1977.

23 See A. Rowe (1971), p.65.

24 D.M. Scott (1964), p.326.

25 P.J. Phelan (1973), p.74.

26 J.A. Simpson (1973), also Council for Cultural Co-operation (1965).

27 P.J. Phelan (1973), p.74.

28 Scottish Education Department Circular 296, 4 December 1954.

29 Scottish Education Department Circular 436, 16 May 1960. See also DES Circular 2/70 (February 1970) 'Chance to Share' and Schools Council (1971) which stressed: 'The advantage to be gained through co-operative use of buildings and their amenities include not only the added resources available to the youth centre but the value to the school of additional social accommodation for the older pupils' p.8.

30 B. Bernstein and B. Davies (1969), p.77.

31 *Trends in Education* (April 1967), p.31.

32 J.A. Nettleton and D.J. Moore (1967), p.11.

33 B. Stewart (1970), p.74.

34 P. Clyne (1972), p.133.

35 A. Fairbairn (1971), *Times Educational Supplement* 27 August 1971. See also B. Taylor (1975).

36 Final Report of the Adult Education Committee of the Ministry of Reconstruction. Cmnd 321 (1919), para. 168.

37 J.M. Hogan (1968), p.14. J.B. Mays (1967) p.6, makes much the same point in calling for the introduction into the classroom 'of something of a freedom and elan of the Youth Service at its best'.

38 R. Aitken (1975).

39 See for a full discussion of the role of community work in a school setting C. Ball and M. Ball (1973).

40 G. Smith and T. Smith (1974), p.190.

41 J. Rennie (1977), p.22.

42 N. Postman (1970), p.244.

43 A. Griffith (1978), p.10.

44 J.B. Mays (1965), p.12. Henry Morris (1925), p.23, in similar vein, hoped that 'The village college would provide the chance for creating for the countryside a new type of village leader and teacher

with a wide function embracing human welfare in its highest sense – spiritual, physical, social and economic.'

45 R. Aitken (1975), p.575. A.G. Powell (1974), p.162, argues that community schools 'responding to local needs would help immigrant communities to integrate more effectively . . . and also remove much of the need for a protective mechanism against the "outside world" amongst ethnic minorities.'

46 E. Midwinter (1972), p.189.

47 P.J. Phelan (1973), p.225, quotes one example of this control function in operation. An area youth officer describes how various pressures were brought to bear on a youth tutor in his area, to make him exclude from his youth club and activities any pupils who were involved in external examination courses so as to ensure that they would concentrate solely on their studies.

48 P.J. Phelan (1973), p.100. The headmaster of one community school once described his youth tutor to the author of this study 'as his eyes and ears', who could as a consequence of informal contacts made in the youth club provide him with enough information 'to spot trouble even before it occurred'.

49 I. Illich (1973), p.15. A process that I. Lister (1976), p.17, describes as 'The megalomaniac schemes of the schoolmen who tried to create schools which encapsulated the world.' For Illich's comments on adult education in particular see I. Illich and E. Verne (1976).

50 T. Rogers (1974), p.4. To get around and over this seemingly intractable problem, Rogers was obliged to define the community served by the College simply as 'those members of the public who wish to make use of the Bosworth College for any educational or recreational purpose at any time.'

51 P. Ackroyd (1970), p.34.

52 B. Stewart (1976), p.73.

53 P. Freire (1972), pp.46–7.

54 B. Jackson (1975), *Education Guardian*, 23 September 1975.

55 E. Hutchinson (1974), p.144.

56 See G. Rees and P.T. Edmunds (1971), pp.161–4.

57 J. Eggleston (1976), p.108. T. Holland (1976), also shows how the social divisions within a school may be replicated in patterns of evening usuage amongst pupils.

58 G. John (1977), 'Blaming the Victim', *Times Educational Supplement*, 1 July 1977.

59 YSIC (1972). Like its predecessor the Hunt Report – 'Immigrants and the Youth Service' (HMSO 1967) – the YSIC Report argued, although with many more reservations for 'a multi-racial and integrationist approach . . . and viewed separate provision as desirable only as a precursor to mixed facilities.' p.1. A more recent CRC Report published in 1977 notes concerning the Hunt Report that it 'was generally recognised as having been overtaken by events' (p.20) and goes on to confirm the worst fears of the YSIC report regarding the longevity of separate provision.

60 Community Relations Commission (1977), p.7.
61 B. Hill (1972), 'Youngsters Give Multi-Racial Clubs the Cold Shoulder', *Times Educational Supplement,* 26 May 1975.
62 J. Haworth (1975), p.282.
63 J. Trenaman (1967) concluded that approximately 40 per cent of the adult population are actually hostile to the very idea of education. This attitude largely resulted from their own experience of school and clearly puts them beyond the reach of most formal educational provision.
64 M. Bone and E. Ross (1972), p.51.
65 M.H. Bristow (1970), p.221. See also P. Jephcott (1967), L.B. Hendry and D.O. Simpson (1977).
66 H. Webb (1972), p.8.
67 N. Parry and J. Flowers (1972), p.13.
68 J.A. Simpson (1970), p.403.
69 R.S. Peters (1966), p.193.
70 See F. Musgrave and P.H. Taylor (1969). They conclude that 'in England education today, what is still remarkable is not the power of clients (whether pupils or their parents) but their impotence' (p.11). Also R.J. McCloy (1974), special reference to community schools.
71 P.J. Blackmore (1975), p.439. A. Fairbairn (1974), p.10 supports this view, stating that 'the overall executive control of the warden-principal is of absolute and cardinal importance.' Gwent appears to be the only LEA to have split the control of the campus between a Headteacher (day) and a Manager responsible for evening and week-end usage. See T. Morgan (1975), p.229.
72 G. Baron (1970), p.5. J.B. Mays (1970), pp.43–4, 'The Head of the English School is still traditionally a fairly isolated figure of elevated power, and one can only wonder how long this state of affairs will be allowed to continue . . . . Someday . . . (he) must yield to a more rational and democratic arrangement of power.'
73 P. Berger and L. Luckmann (1971), p.4.
74 R. Williams (1961), p.169.
75 A. Etzioni (1961), p.109.
76 See for example W. Waller (1965), p.196.
77 G. Noble (1970), p.329.
78 B. Doswell (1974), pp.1–2.
79 See R.J. McCloy (1974), who examines in some detail the management structure of Cambridgeshire Community Colleges.
80 B. Doswell (1974), p.2.
81 A. Tweedie *et al.* (1973), p.60.
82 R.S. Peters (1959), p.52.
83 P.J. Phelan (1973), p.211.
84 Ibid., p.233.
85 E. Venables (1971), p.69, illustrates this point in the following account of an interview with 'the "well-known" headmaster of an outstanding liberal school who said . . . that in his view the youth club, which had been built very near to the school, should be

separately administered. He wanted schooling and what went with
on in the club clearly differentiated. To him and many others like
him teaching is a profession which commits him to a clearly defined
and limited role in relation to his pupils. He is not a parent and he
is not responsible for what pupils do in their leisure time.'

86 Quoted by D.T. Elias (1971), p.67.
87 E. Venables (1971), p.13.
88 E. Venables (1971), p.68.
89 D.T. Elias (1971), p.47.
90 Salary scales vary widely between different LEAs and even within
    individual LEAs according to their evaluation of a particular post.
    A survey of school based youth posts advertised in the *Times
    Educational Supplement* during the first three months of 1978
    revealed that 32 per cent were offered at Burnham Scale 3, 24 per
    cent at Burnham F.E. Lec.I, 16 per cent at J.N.C. Scale 3, 16 per
    cent at J.N.C. Scale 2, 8 per cent at Burnham Scale 2 and the
    remainder were equally divided between F.E. Lec.II and Burnham
    Scale 4.
91 L. Button (1970), p.7.
92 P. Hayman (1970), p.3.
93 H. Morris (1925), p.21.
94 D.T. Elias (1971), p.80.
95 See E. Hutchinson (1974) and D.O. Wright (1975).
96 R.P.W. Mayes (1973), p.12.
97 C.F. Palfrey and J.B. Thomas (1972), p.101-2. Confirmed by
    A. Tweedie *et al.* (1973) who report that young people interviewed
    'did not see the Further Education Centre as being separate from
    day teaching', p.20.
98 L.B. Hendry and D.O. Simpson (1977), p.118-9.
99 Education Digest (1976), p.3.
100 Schools Council (1971), p.8.

Chapter 5 Spreading the load

1 F. Booton (1977), p.9.
2 See for example B. Davies (1976), p.570, J. Ewen (1974), *Times
   Educational Supplement* 12 July 1974, R. Woolfe (1971). One
   Westhill survey puts affiliation as low as 9 per cent quoted by
   D. Howell (1971), p.6.
3 Some LEAs have unilaterally introduced their own upper and lower
   age limits; Northumberland has for example adopted an age range
   of 13 to 18. Other LEAs have allowed leaders to enrol members
   below 14 at their discretion or alternatively set up 'Junior Clubs'.
4 A. Tweedie *et al.* (1973), p.44.
5 See M. Thomas and J. Perry (1975), p.58.
6 HMSO (1969), p.1.
7 HMSO (1969), p.2.
8 YSIC (undated).
9 D.E. Ince (1971), p.64.

10 N. Parry and J. Flowers (1972), p.11.
11 There is a remarkable correlation between the results of the Parry and Flowers survey and that of M. Bone and E. Ross (1972), p.24; the former found that 92 per cent of young people try at least one youth group and the latter put the figure at 93 per cent.
12 J. Eggleston (1976), p.107.
13 M.R. Farrant and H.J. Marchant (1977), p.2.
14 J. Storry (1972), p.14.
15 M. Gardner (1974), provides a comprehensive survey of experimental youth work projects 1960–74.
16 M.L. Hening *et al.* (1977), p.2.
17 Ibid., p.6. A number of detailed reports of unattached youth projects have been published, see H.M. Olden (1972); D.E. Ince (1971); C. Smith, M. Farrant and H. Marchant (1974); A. Cox and G. Cox (1977) and N. Collins and L. Hoggarth (1977).
18 K. Marks (1977), p.11. J. Eggleston (1976), p.149 puts the proportion of unattached workers as high as 30 per cent but this is not supported by the presentation of any evidence. Marks's estimate is based on considerable research and is probably the more realistic estimate.
19 'Education', *Digest on the Youth Service,* 7 September 1976.
20 J. Ewen (1974), *Times Educational Supplement* 12 July 1974.
21 Ibid.
22 N. Parry and J. Flowers (1972), p.13.
23 L. Blackmore (1973), p.10.
24 D. Jackson (1973), p.15.
25 M. Bacon (1977), reviews the history behind the appointment of these two field workers and their achievements and failures.
26 D. Ward (1977), pp.10–11.
27 'Youth Service' (1977), p.4.
28 B. Davies (1975), *Times Educational Supplement* 21 February 1975.
29 C. Andrews (1977), p.1.
30 See E. Younghusband (1951), pp.62–8.
31 NCSS (1971), p.19.
32 HMSO (1968), para. 474–501.
33 See A. Tweedie (1974) and J. Baker (1977). An example of how extensive some of the projects have become can be gauged from the following report, 'Intermediate Treatment, which can be a requirement placed on a youngster supervised by the court or be undertaken voluntarily . . . can also have a great impact in preventing children "at risk" becoming anti-social or delinquent as they grow up. Gateshead is providing a new idea in intermediate treatment . . . by establishing a centre . . . . It is planned to use the farm all the year round and it will also be open for other children in Gateshead . . . (offering) . . . camp-sites, aerial rope ways, army style assault courses, orienteering and an open air area for sports and games. About two acres of land will be used for growing crops on a strip system of agriculture and the farm buildings will be restored and put to use', *Gateshead News,* January 1978.

34   D. Carter (1973), p.11.
35   A.P. Miles (1954) quoted by R. Plant (1970), p.6. A more recent exposition of this view in a standard social work text can be found in R. Foren and R. Bailey (1968), p.18.
36   N. Bond (1971), p.22.
37   The precise status of social workers has been a matter of considerable debate regarding whether they should be classified as full professionals or mere semi-professionals, see for example N. Toren (1972), R. Hamilton (1974).
38   P. Hall (1976), pp.128-9.
39   J.R. Watts and T.A. Whitworth (1968), p.19.
40   P. Polish (1971), p.8.
41   D. Thorpe (1972), p.35.
42   S. Rees (1975), p.69. D. Thorpe (1972), p.25, illustrates this point in his description of the priorities that were applied during the 'Ryehill' project, 'Young people in the area who were able to fit into and use conventional clubs could cross the railway line into Risefield, priority would not, therefore, be given to this type of facility.'
43   M.R. Farrant and H.J. Marchant (1970), p.3.
44   M. Davies (1976), p.87.
45   *Newcastle Evening Chronicle*, 21 October 1977.
46   Six pilot areas were originally chosen and the first one of these began operating in Notthinghamshire in 1973.
47   M. L. Smyth (1978), p.11.
48   J. Harding (1974), p.481.
49   HMSO (1968), p.217.
50   In 1972 the Avon County Council actually proposed the transfer of responsibility for its youth provision from the Education Department to Parks and Leisure. This move was blocked by the DES.
51   In 1976 North Tyneside recruited 40 young persons, including 10 unemployed teachers to work on its playschemes, under the Job Creation Programme (JCP). North Tyneside Community Development Project (1977), p.86.
52   *Youth Service*, no.8, April 1976.
53   *Times Educational Supplement* editorial, 21 April 1978.
54   See for example D. MacDonald (1976), pp.13-14.
55   'After Six' (1975).
56   'Springboard' (1977), p.5.
57   B. Davies (1977), p.6.
58   M. Bacon (1977), p.5.
59   A. Tweedie *et al.* (1973), p.49.
60   J. Nixon (1973), p.37.
61   J. Eggleston (1976), pp.7-27.
62   F. Booton (1977), pp.9-10.

Conclusion

1   R. Charlton (1972), p.8.

2   Warwickshire County Council internal policy document on the Youth Service, June 1971. Approved by Council 16 June 1977.
3   'Education', *Digest on the Youth Service*, 17 September, p.4.
4   G. Ette (1972), p.4.
5   D. Howell (1971), p.5.
6   Little has actually been written or produced on the curriculum of the youth club; the value and relative merits of various activities are totally ignored in journals, books and pamphlets. An individual might read almost all that has been written on youth work in Britain during the last twenty years and be no wiser as to what happens in them. Exceptions to this rule include S.C. Hedges (1961); K.R. Matthews (1975); National Youth Bureau (1975).
7   M. Tax (1972), p.25.
8   J. Ewen (1972a), p.27.
9   Report of the Committee on the Age of Majority, July 1967, Cmnd. 3342.
10 F.W. Musgrove (1964), p.123.
11 P.H.K. Kuenstler (1955), p.74.
12 P. Abrams and A. Little (1965), p.331. See also F. Parkin (1970).
13 *Youth Service*, 14 March 1977 (No.19), p.1. The Youth Service was not the only educational area to receive scant attention as Oxtoby notes 'The so-called "great educational debate" has been concerned almost exclusively with compulsory schooling – the curriculum, assessment of standards, the education and training of teachers, links between school and working life. Further and adult education have received hardly a mention.' N. Oxtoby (1978), p.355.
14 F. Milson (1971), *Times Educational Supplement*, 30 January 1971.
15 A.N. Fairbairn (1976), p.71.
16 National Association of Youth and Community Education Officers – Evidence to the Layfield Committee on Local Government Finance, 'Education' 18 April 1975, p.422.
17 F. Booton (1977), p.10.
18 A.N. Fairbairn (1909), p.339.
19 J.A. Simpson (1970), p.43.
20 For perhaps the fullest exposition of this proposition see J. Ewen (1972), pp.12–13.
21 *New Society* Special Report (1977), p.289. See also W.W. Daniel and E. Stilgoe (1977).
22 See for example J. Monahan, 'Life among the Young Unemployed Persons', *Sunday Times*, 31 July 1977.
23 J.B. Mays (1955), p.29.
24 C. Poster (1977), p.9.

Bibliography

The named publisher refers to the edition quoted; in many cases this was not the original publisher.

Abrams, M., *Teenage Consumer Spending*, London Exchange Press, 1959.

Abrams, M., 'Facts on the Earnings and Spendings of the Teenage Consumer', in *Trends in the Services for Youth*, edited by J.H. Leicester and J. Farndale, Pergamon, 1967.

Abrams, M. and Rose, R., *Must Labour Lose?* Penguin, 1960.

Abrams, P., 'The Failure of Social Reform 1918-1920', *Past and Present*, no.24, 1963.

Abrams, P. and Little, A., 'The Young Activist in British Politics', *British Journal of Sociology*, vol.17, 1965.

Ackroyd, P., 'Youth and Community Centres for the Future', *Youth Review*, vol.19, 1970.

Adelman, C., *Generations*, Penguin, 1973.

'After Six', *The First Two Years 1972-1974*, After Six Housing Advisory Service Trust Ltd, Tyssen Road, London, 1975.

Aitken, R., 'Combating Loneliness in the Big City', *Education*, vol.145, 1975.

Anderson, J.C., *Participants in Part-time Youth Work Training*, National Youth Bureau, 1975.

Andrews, C., 'Getting I.T. Going', *Social Work Today*, vol.8, 1977.

Armstrong, G. and Wilson, M., 'City Politics and Deviancy Amplification' in *Politics and Deviance*, edited by I. Taylor and L. Taylor, Penguin, 1973.

Ashworth, W., *A Short History of the International Economy*, Longmans, 1952.

Ashworth, W., *An Economic History of England 1870-1939*, Methuen, 1960.

Aves, G.M., *The Voluntary Worker in the Social Services,* Report of a Committee jointly set up by the NCSS and NISWT, Allen & Unwin, 1969.

Bacon, M., 'The Realities and the Challenge', *Youth Service*, no.7, 1977.

Baden-Powell, R., *Scouting and Youth Movements*, Ernest Benn, 1929.

Baden-Powell, R., *Scouting for Boys*, Pearson, 1937 and 1963.

Baker, J., 'Applying Community Development Principles to Youth Work', *Community Development Journal* vol.12, 1977.

Ball, C. and Ball, M., *Education for a Change*, Penguin, 1973.

Bantock, G.H., 'Progressivism and the Content of Education', in *Black Paper 1975 - The Fight for Education*, edited by C.B. Cox and R. Boyson, Dent, 1975.

Barnes, L.J., *The Outlook for Youth Work*, King George's Jubilee Trust, 1948.

Barnsley, M., 'Training for Youth Work', *Youth Review*, vol.25, 1972.

Baron, G., 'An Overview' in *Headship in the 70s*, edited by B. Allen, Blackwell, 1970.

Batten, T.R., *The Non-Directive Approach in Group and Community Work*, Oxford University Press, 1967.

Bell, V.A., *Junior Instruction Centres and their Future*, Carnegie United Kingdom Trust, Edinburgh, 1934.

Benewick, R., *The Fascist Movement in Britain*, Allen Lane, 1972.

Berger, P. and Luckmann, T., *The Social Construction of Reality*, Penguin, 1971.

Bernstein, B. and Davies, B., 'Some Sociological Comments on Plowden' in *Perspectives on Plowden*, edited by R.S. Peters, Routledge & Kegan Paul, 1969.

Birch, A.E., *The Story of the Boys' Brigade*, Muller, 1959.

Blackburn, R., 'Inequality and Exploitation', *New Left Review*, no.42, 1967.

Blackmore, L., 'Intermediate Treatment – Ridiculous', *Youth Service*, vol.12, 1973.

Blackmore, P.J., 'From the Known, Gradually to the Unknown', *Education*, vol.145, 1975.

Bond, N., 'The Case for Radical Casework', *Social Work Today*, vol. 2, no.9, 1971.

Bone, M. and Ross, E., *The Youth Service and Similar Provision for Young People*, HMSO, 1972.

Booton, F., 'Administration by Afterthought', *Youth in Society*, April 1976.

Booton, F., 'De-Schooling the Youth Service', *Youth Service*, no.8, 1977.

Brew, J. Macalister, *Informal Education*, Faber, 1944.

Brew, J. Macalister, *Youth and Youth Groups*, Faber, 1957.

Bristow, M.H., 'The Role of the Youth Worker in Contemporary Society', unpublished M.Ed. thesis, University of Leicester, 1970.

Burns, J., 'News Review – October 1889', reprinted in *Strikes*, edited by R. Frow, E. Frow and M. Katnaka, Charles Knight (1971), 1889.

Button, L., *Training for Youth Work in Colleges of Education*, University College of Swansea, 1969.

Button, L., 'Training for School-Based Youth Work' in *Debate*, published by Youth Service Information Centre, Leicester, 1970.

Byrne, E.M., 'Inequality in Education – Discriminal Resource – Allocation in Schools?' *Education Review*, vol.27, no.3, 1975.

Calouste Gulbenkian, *Community Work and Social Change*, Longman, 1968.

Cameron, C., Lush, A. and Meara, G., *Disinherited Youth*, Carnegie United Kingdom Trust, Edinburgh, 1943.

Carter, D., 'The Role of Social Services in Work with Young People', *Youth in Society*, no.2, 1973.

Charlton, R., 'The Role of the Youth Officer', *Youth Service*, vol.12, no.1, 1972.

Chibnall, S., 'Law and Order News', Tavistock Publications, 1977.
Chivers, T.S., *Which Way for Youth Workers?*, National Youth Bureau, 1977.
Clarke, J., 'Reconceptualising Youth Culture', unpublished M.A. thesis, University of Birmingham, 1974.
Clarke, J., Hall, S., Jefferson, T. and Roberts, B., 'Subcultures, Cultures and Class' in *Resistance Through Rituals* edited by Hall, S. and Jefferson, T., Hutchinson, 1975.
Clemans, M., 'Youth Worker in Teacher Training', *Trends in Education*, vol.1, no.2, 1966.
Clyne, P., *The Disadvantaged Adult: Educational and Social Needs of Minority Groups*, Longman, 1972.
Coburn, O., *Youth Hostel Story*, National Council of Social Service, 1950.
Cohen, A., *Delinquent Boys*, Free Press, USA, 1955.
Cohen, S., *Folk Devils and Moral Panics*, Paladin, 1973.
Cohn-Bendit, D., *Obsolete Communism –The Left Wing Alternative*, Penguin, 1969.
Coleman, J., *The Adolescent Society*, Free Press, USA, 1961.
Collins, N. and Hoggarth, L., *No Man's Landmarks*, National Youth Bureau, 1977.
Collins, R., 'Functional and Conflict Theories of Educational Stratification', *American Sociological Review*, vol.36, 1971.
Collis, H., Hazelwood, R. and Hurll, F., *B – P's Scouts*, Collins, 1961.
Community Relations Commission, 'Seen but not Served', published by Youth Section CRC, Bedford Street, London, 1977.
Council for Cultural Co-operation, *Leisure-time Facilities for Young People From 13 to 25 years of Age*, Strasbourg, 1965.
Cox, A. and Cox, G., *Borderlines*, National Youth Bureau, 1977.
Crossman, R., 'None So Fair as can Compare with the British Volunteer', *The Times*, 8 August 1973.
Curtis, S.J. and Boultwood, M.E.A., *History of English Education Since 1800*, University Tutorial Press, 1960.
Daniel, W.W. and Stilgoe, E., *Where are They Now? – a follow-up study of the unemployed*, PEP Report, no.572, 1977.
Davies, B., 'Non-Swinging Youth', *New Society*, vol.14, 1969.
Davies, B., 'Youth Club Users', *New Society*, 16 December 1976.
Davies, B., 'Youth Cultures Myths and Political Realities', *Youth in Society*, no.16, 1976a.
Davies, B., 'Agency Collaboration or Worker Control?', *Youth in Society*, no.22, 1977.
Davies, B., 'From Hope to Perplexity', *Times Educational Supplement*, 21 February 1975.
Davies, B. and Gibson, A., *The Social Education of the Adolescent*, University of London Press, 1967.
Davies, L. and Meighan, R., 'Review of Schooling and Sex Roles', *Educational Review*, vol.27, 1975.
Davies, M., 'A Tale of Two Perspectives: Defensive or Developmental?', *Probation Journal*, vol.23, no.23, 1976.

Davies, K., 'The Sociology of Parent–Youth Conflict', *American Sociological Review*, August 1940, vol.5, 1940.

Dawes, F., *A Cry from the Streets*, Wayland, 1975.

Day, M., *A Review of the Training Brochures of a Number of Authorities in the London and Home Counties Region*, a consultative document prepared by the Brunel Institute of Organisation and Social Studies for the Regional Training Consultative Unit, 1973.

Dearling, A., 'The Theory and Practice of Youth Work in One Large Youth Centre', *Youth in Society*, no.2, 1973.

Derbyshire Education Authority, *Memorandum on Social Education*, Derby, 1967.

Doswell, B., 'Who Needs Forty Year Olds Anyway', *National Youth Bureau*, Occasional Paper no.2, 1974.

Downes, D., *The Delinquent Solution*, Routledge & Kegan Paul, 1966.

Durant, H., *The Problem of Leisure*, Routledge & Kegan Paul, 1938.

Eager, W.M., *Making Men*, London University Press, 1953.

Education, 'Evidence to the Layfield Committee', 18 April 1975.

Education, 'Service of Youth Digest', 7 September 1976.

Eggleston, J., *Adolescence and Community*, Arnold, 1976.

Eisenstadt, S.N., *From Generation to Generation*, Free Press, USA, 1956.

Elias, D.T., 'Role Conflict in a Community College Setting', unpublished thesis for Diploma in Sociology and Psychology of Education, University of Leicester, 1971.

Elvin, L., 'The Positive Roles of Society and the Teacher' in *Perspectives on Plowden*, edited by R.S. Peters, Routledge & Kegan Paul, 1969.

Ensor, R.C.K., *England 1870–1914*, Clarendon Press, 1936.

Epperson, D.C., 'A Re-assessment of Indices of Parental Influence in the Adolescent Society', *American Sociological Review*, vol.29, 1964.

Erickson, M.L. and Empey, L.T., 'Class Position, Peers and Delinquency', *Sociology and Social Research*, no.49, 1965.

Ette, G., *For Youth Only*, Faber, 1949.

Ette, G., 'Inequality of Opportunity', *Youth Review*, no.23, 1972.

Etzioni, A., *A Comparative Analysis of Complex Organisations*, Free Press, USA, 1961.

Evans, W.H., *Young People in Society*, Blackwell, 1965.

Ewen, J., *Towards a Youth Policy*, MBS (Leicester), 1972.

Ewen, J., 'Should Youth Workers be Peaceful Revolutionaries or Agents of Conformity', *Youth Review*, no.24, 1972a.

Ewen, J., *A Positive Future for the Youth Service*, National Youth Bureau, 1975.

Eysenck, H., 'The Technology of Consent', *New Scientist*, 26 June 1969.

Fairbairn, A., 'New Methods and Aids in Community Colleges', *Times Educational Supplement*, 27 August 1971.

Fairbairn, A.N., 'Youth Service in a Community School', *Adult Education*, vol.41, no.6, 1969.

Fairbairn, A.N. 'Community Education – the Next Ten Years', *Youth in Society*, no.3, 1974.

Fairbairn, A.N., 'In-Service Training Needs of the Community College', *British Journal of In-Service Education*, vol.2, no.2, 1976.

Farrant, M.R. and Marchant, H.J., *Making Contact with Unreached Youth*, Youth Development Trust, 1971.

Fisher, R., 'The Contribution of Colleges of Education' in *Training for Full-time Youth and Community Workers – A Consultative Document*, National Youth Bureau, 1975.

Foren, R. and Bailey, R., *Authority in Social Casework*, Pergamon, 1968.

Foster, J., *Class Struggle and the Industrial Revolution*, Weidenfeld & Nicolson, 1974.

Fountain, N., 'The Festival of the Oppressed' reprinted in *The Left in Britain 1956–1968* edited by D. Widgery (1976), Penguin, 1978.

Fraser, D., *The Evolution of the British Welfare State*, Macmillan, 1973.

Frease, D., 'Delinquency, Social Class and the Schools', *Sociology and Social Research*, vol.57, 1972–3.

Freire, R., *Pedagogy of the Oppressed*, Penguin, 1972.

Fyvel, T.R., *The Insecure Offenders*, Penguin, 1961.

Gamble, A. and Walton, P., *Capitalism in Crisis*, Macmillan, 1976.

Gardner, M., *Developmental Work with Young People*, National Youth Bureau, 1974.

Gateshead News, 'Treatment for Youngsters in Trouble', 1 January 1978.

Gibbon, F.P., *William Smith of the Boys Brigade*, Collins, 1934.

Gibson, N.J., 'Monetary, Credit and Fiscal Policies' in *The U.K. Economy*, edited by A.R. Prest, Weidenfeld & Nicolson, 1966.

Godby, V. and Key, P., 'College Leavers – Where do they go?', *Youth in Society*, no.11, 1975.

Goffman, E., *The Presentation of Self in Everyday Life*, Penguin, 1959.

Goldthorpe, J.H. and Bevan, P., 'The Study of Social Stratification in Great Britain: 1946–1976', *Social Science Information*, no.16, 1977.

Goodwin, Sir R., *A Matter of Faith*, National Association of Boys' Clubs, 1973.

Gosden, P.H.J.H., *Self-Help*, Batsford, 1973.

Graves, R. and Hodge, A., *The Long Weekend*, Faber, 1955.

Greenberg, D.F., 'Delinquency and the Age Structure of Society', *Contemporary Crises*, vol.1, no.2, 1977.

Griffith, A., 'Youth Action – Community Service in Schools, a Missed Opportunity', *Youth in Society*, no.27, 1978.

Hadfield, J.A., *Childhood and Adolescence*, Penguin, 1962.

Halevy, E., *History of the English People in the Nineteenth Century*, vol.5, Benn, 1951.

Hall, P., *Reforming the Welfare*, Heinemann, 1976.

Halliday, F., 'Students of the World Unite' in *Student Power*, edited by A. Cockburn and R. Blackburn, Penguin, 1969.

Hamblett, C. and Deverson, J., *Generation X*, Tandem Books, 1964.

Hamilton, R., 'The Tentacles of Authority and Control', *Youth Review*, no.24, 1972.

Hamilton, R., 'Social Work: an Aspiring Profession and its Difficulties', *British Journal of Social Work*, vol.4, 1974.

Hannington, W., *Unemployed Struggles 1919–1936*, Lawrence & Wishart, 1977.

Hanmer, J., *Girls at Leisure*, London Union of Youth Clubs, 1964.

Hanson, D., 'Community Centres and their Functions as Educational Institutions and Agencies for Social Control', *Durham Review*, no.28, 1972.

Harding, J., 'The Offender and the Community', *Social Work Today*, vol.5, 1974.

Hargreaves, D., 'Social Relations in Secondary School', Routledge & Kegan Paul, 1967.

Hasenfield, Y., 'The Role of Employment Placement Services in Maintaining Poverty', *Social Service Review*, vol.49, no.4, 1975.

Hawes, D., *Young People Today*, National Council of Social Service, 1966.

Haworth, J., 'Towards a More Genuine Sense of Involvement', *Education*, vol.145, 1975.

Hayman, P., 'The School Based Youth Worker', *Youth Service*, vol.10, no.5, 1970.

Haywood, H., 'The Role of the Professional Youth Worker', *Youth Service*, vol.11, no.4, 1971.

Hechinger, G. and Hechinger, G.M., *Teenage Tyranny*, Duckwood, 1964.

Hedges, S.G., *Youth Club Programmes*, Methuen, 1961.

Hendry, L.B. and Simpson, D.O., 'One Centre: Two Sub-Cultures', *Scottish Educational Studies*, vol.9, 1977.

Hening, M. *et al.*, 'Evaluation of Detached Youth Work', National Youth Bureau, 1977.

Henry, J., *Culture against Man*, Penguin, 1972.

Herbert, S.M., *Britain's Health*, Penguin, 1939.

Heussenstamm, F.K., 'Bumper Stickers and the Cops' in *Social Psychology of Everyday Life*, edited by P.G. Swingle (1971), Penguin, 1973.

Hill, B., 'Youngsters Give Multi-Racial Clubs the Cold Shoulder', *Times Educational Supplement*, 26 May 1975.

Hobsbawm, E.J., *The Age of Revolution 1789–1848*, Mentor, USA, 1962.

Hobsbawm, E.J., *Industry and Empire*, Penguin, 1969.

Hogan, J.M., *The Relationship between the Youth Service and Secondary Schools*, University of Leeds, Institute of Education, 1968.

Holland, J.A., 'Parental Involvement in an Evolving Community School', unpublished B.Phil. thesis, University of York, 1976.

Hopper, E. and Osborn, M., *Adult Students; Education, Selection and Social Control*, Frances Pinter, 1973.

Horowitz, I.L. and Liebowitz, M., 'Social Deviance and Political Marginality', *Social Problems*, vol.15, no.3, 1968.

Howell, D., 'How the Government Killed Community Service', *Youth Review*, no.20, 1971.

Hutchinson, E., 'Participation in the Leicestershire Community Colleges', *Studies in Adult Education*, no.6, 1974.

Illich, I., *De-Schooling Society*, Penguin, 1973.

Illich, I. and Verne, E., *Imprisoned in a Global Classroom*, Readers and Writers Cooperative, 1976.

Ince, D.E., *Contact*, Youth Service Information Centre, Leicester, 1971.

Jackson, B., 'The Case for an Open College', the *Guardian*, 23 September 1975.

Jackson, B. and Marsden, D., *Education and the Working Class*, Penguin, 1962.

Jackson, D., 'Scout Association and Intermediate Treatment', *Youth Service*, vol.12, no.6, 1973.

Jefferson, T., 'Cultural Responses of the Teds' in *Resistance Through Rituals* edited by S. Hall and T. Jefferson, Hutchinson, 1976.

Jencks, C. *et al.*, *Inequality*, Penguin, 1972.

Jephcott, P., *Time of One's Own*, Oliver & Boyd, 1967.

John, G., 'Blaming the Victim', *Times Educational Supplement*, 1 July 1977.

Jones, H.A., 'Report on the Feedback' in National Youth Bureau Consultative Document *Training for Full-time Youth and Community Workers*, 1975.

Keniston, K., *The Uncommitted*, Harcourt Brace Jovanovich, USA, 1960.

King George's Jubilee Trust, *Youth Service Tomorrow*, Ashridge Report, 1951.

King George's Jubilee Trust, *Citizens of Tomorrow*, 1955.

Kuenstler, P.H.K., 'Voluntary Youth Leaders', University of Bristol Institute of Education Publication no.5, University of London Press, 1953.

Kuenstler, P.H.K., 'Spontaneous Youth Groups', University of Bristol Institute of Education Publications no.8, University of London Press, 1955.

Lacey, C., *Hightown Grammar*, Manchester University Press, 1970.

Larkin, R., 'Youth Club or Palais?', *Youth Service*, vol.12, no.3, 1970.

Layton-Henry, Z., 'Labour's Lost Youth', *Journal of Contemporary History*, vol.11, 1976.

Leeson, C., *The Child and the War*, Howard Association, 1917.

Levitan, S.A. and Taggart, R., *The Job Crisis for Black Youth*, Praeger, USA, 1971.

Lindsay, K., 'What Went Wrong with the Youth Service', *Times Educational Supplement*, 1 August 1975.

Lister, I., 'De-Schooling Revisited' in *After De-Schooling What?* by I. Illich, Writers and Readers Publishing Cooperative, 1976.

Livingstone, J.M., *Britain and the World Economy*, Penguin, 1966.

Loewe, L., *Basil Henriques*, Routledge & Kegan Paul, 1976.

Lovett, T., *Adult Education, Community Development and the Working Class*, Ward Lock, 1973.

Lowe, J., *Adult Education in England and Wales*, Michael Joseph, 1970.

Lunnon, V.M., 'Self Discovery through Adventure – Outward Bound Trust' in *Trends in the Services for Youth* edited by J.H. Leicester and J. Farndall, Pergamon, 1967.

Macadam, E., *The New Philanthropy*, Allen & Unwin, 1934.

McCloy, R.J., 'Community Colleges – Their First 50 Years and the Corporate Ideal', *Local Government Studies,* June and October, 1974.

MacDonald, D., 'Crossing Agency Boundaries', *Youth in Society*, no.18, 1976.

McLuhan, M., *Counterblast*, Rapp & Whiting, 1970.

Mailer, N., 'The White Negro' in *Protest* edited by G. Feldman and M. Gartenberg, Panther Books, 1957.

Mailer, N., *Miami and the Siege of Chicago*, Penguin, 1969.

Mandel, H., 'The Changing Role of the Bourgeois University', reprinted in *Counter Course* (1972) edited by T. Pateman, Penguin, 1970.

Marcuse, H., *An Essay on Liberation*, Penguin, 1969.

Marks, K., 'Detached Youth Work Practice', *Youth in Society*, no.20, 1977.

Marshall, T.H., *Social Policy*, Hutchinson, 1975.

Marsland, D. and Day, M., *The Youth Service and its Continuing Development*, National Youth Bureau, 1975.

Marsland, D. and Hunter, P., 'Youth – a Real Force and an Essential Concept', *Youth in Society*, no.18, 1976.

Marwick, A., *The Deluge,* Penguin, 1967.

Matthews, K.R., *A Guide to Youth Club Leadership*, Elek, 1975.

Mayes, R.P.W., 'The Process of Maturation at Rawlins Community College During the First Five Years', unpublished thesis for the Post-Graduate Diploma in Educational Studies, University of Leicester, 1973.

Mays, J.B., 'Street Football: Results of a Liverpool Survey' in *Spontaneous Youth Groups* edited by P.H.K. Kuenstler, University of Bristol Institute of Education Publication No.8, University of London Press, 1955.

Mays, J.B., *Education and the Urban Child*, Liverpool University Press, 1962.

Mays, J.B., *The Young Pretenders*, Joseph, 1965.

Mays, J.B., *The School in its Social Setting*, Longman, 1967.

Mays, J.B., 'The Head and the Home' in *Headship in the 1970s* edited by B. Allen, Blackwell, 1968.

Meade, J.E., *Efficiency, Equality and the Ownership of Property*, Allen & Unwin, 1964.

Midwinter, E., *Priority Education*, Penguin, 1972.

Millward, A.S., *The Economic Effects of the World Wars on Britain*, Macmillan, 1970.

Milson, F., *Youth Work in the 1970s*, Routledge & Kegan Paul, 1970.

Milson, F., 'Future of the Youth Service', *Times Educational Supplement*, 12 March 1971.

Milson, F., 'Destiny of the Youth Service', *Times Educational Supplement*, 30 April 1971.

Mitchell, B.R. and Jones, H., *Second Abstract of British Historical Statistics*, Cambridge University Press, 1971.

Morgan, A.E., *Needs of Youth*, Oxford University Press, 1939.

Morgan, T., 'Sharing Means More Than Joint Use', *Education*, vol.145, no.9, 1975.

Morris, H., *The Village College*, Cambridge University Press, 1925.

Morse, M., *The Unattached*, Penguin, 1965.

Murdock, G. and McCron, R., 'Youth and Class: The Career of a Confusion' in *Working Class Youth Culture* edited by G. Mungham and G. Pearson, Routledge & Kegan Paul, 1976.

Murdock, G. and Phelps, G., 'Youth Culture and the School Revisited', *British Journal of Sociology*, vol.23, 1972.

Musgrave, P.W., *Society and Education in England since 1800*, Methuen, 1968.

Musgrave, S. and Taylor, P.H., *Society and the Teacher's Role*, Routledge & Kegan Paul, 1965.

Musgrove, F., *Youth and the Social Order*, Routledge & Kegan Paul, 1964.

National Children's Bureau, *Britain's Sixteen-Year-Olds*, NCB, 1976.

National Council of Public Morals, *The Cinema*, NCPM, 1917.

National Council of Social Service, *Youth in Action*, NCSS, 1971.

National Youth Bureau, 'Curriculum Development in the Youth Club', Occasional Paper, no.11, 1975.

National Youth Bureau, *Training for Full-time Youth and Community Workers*, NYB, 1976.

Nettleton, J.A. and Moore, D.J., *School and Community*, National Institute of Adult Education, 1967.

New Society, 'Special Report – Is Youth Unemployment Really the Problem', vol.42, 1977.

Newcastle Evening Chronicle, '5-a-side boys learn to kick crime habit', 21 October 1977.

Nicholson, R.J., 'The Distribution of Personal Income', *Lloyds Bank Review*, no.83.

Nixon, J., 'The Sleeping Community', *Scottish Journal of Youth and Community Work*, vol.2, no.2, 1973.

Noble, G., 'In Defence of Easterhouses', *New Society*, vol.16, 1970.

North Tyneside Community Development Project, *Unemployment and Youth Workers in North Tyneside*, 1977.

Nuttall, J., *Bomb Culture*, Paladin, 1968.

Olden, H.M., *Hoxton Cafe Project*, Youth Service Information Centre, Leicester, 1972.

Oxford, A., 'Indigenous Leaders and the Re-Deployment of Professionally Trained Workers' in *Training for Full-time Youth and Community Workers*, National Youth Bureau, 1976.

Oxtoby, B., 'Adult Education and Youth Unemployment', *Adult Education*, vol.50, no.6, 1978.

Palfrey, C.F. and Thomas, J.B., 'Adolescent Interest in Adult Education in Community Colleges', *Adult Education*, vol.45, 1972.

Parkin, F., 'Adolescent Status and Student Politics', *Journal of Contemporary History*, vol.5, no.1, 1970.

Parkin, F., *Class, Inequality and the Political Order*, Paladin, 1971.

Parr, J., 'The Role and Professional Identity of Youth Leaders in Statutory and Voluntary Organisations', unpublished M.Ed. thesis, University of Manchester, 1969.

Parr, J., 'The Future Role of the Youth Officer', *Youth Service*, vol.12, no.1, 1972.

Parry, N. and Flowers, J., 'The Class Factor', *Youth Service*, vol.12, no.3, 1972.

Parsons, T., 'Age and Sex in the Social Structure of the U.S.', *American Sociological Review*, no.7, 1942.

Partridge, P.H., 'Politics, Philosophy, Ideology' in *Political Philosophy* edited by A. Quinton, Oxford University Press (1961), 1967.

Paul, L., *Angry Young Man*, Faber, 1950.

Pearson, G., *The Deviant Imagination*, Macmillan, 1975.

Percival, A., *Youth Will be Led*, Collins, 1951.

Perkin, H., *The Origins of Modern English Society 1780-1880*, Routledge & Kegan Paul, 1969.

Peters, R.S., *Authority, Responsibility and Education*, Unwin, 1959.

Peters, R.S., *Ethics and Education*, Unwin, 1966.

Phelan, P.J., 'The Place of Informal Youth Work in Formal Education', unpublished MA thesis, University of Keele, 1973.

Pinker, R., *Social Theory and Social Policy*, Heinemann, 1971.

Plant, R., *Social and Moral Theory in Casework*, Routledge & Kegan Paul, 1970.

Polish, P., 'Open to New Ideas?', *Youth Service*, vol.11, no.4, 1971.

Polk, K. and Pink, W., 'Youth Culture and the School: a Replication', *British Journal of Sociology*, vol.22, 1972.

Pope, R., 'Dole Schools: the North-East Lancashire Experience 1930-1939', *Journal of Educational Administration and History*, vol.4, no.2, 1977.

Poster, C., 'Competitors or Partners? Community Education and the Youth Service', *Youth and Society*, no.25, 1977.

Postman, N., 'The Politics of Reading', *Harvard Educational Review*, vol.40, 1970.

Potter, D.M., *People of Plenty*, University of Chicago Press, 1954.

Powell, A.G., 'The Community School and its Application in the United Kingdom', unpublished M.Ed. thesis, University of Manchester, 1974.

Ralphs, F.L., 'The Affluent Adolescent' in *Trends in the Services for Youth*, edited by J.G. Leicester and J. Farndale, Pergamon, 1967.

Ree, H., *Henry Morris*, Longman, 1973.

Rees, G. and Edmunds, P.T., 'Acacia Avenue and Coronation Street', *Adult Education*, vol.44, 1971.

Rees, S., 'How Misunderstanding Occurs', in *Radical Social Work* edited by R. Bailey and M. Bracke, Arnold, 1975.

Rennie, J., 'Community and Curriculum', *Youth in Society*, no.25, 1977.

Reynolds, E.E., *The Scout Movement*, Oxford University Press, 1950.

Rogers, T., *The Bosworth Papers*, Bosworth Community College, Leicestershire, 1974.

Rooff, M., *Youth and Leisure*, Carnegie United Kingdom Trust, Edinburgh, 1935.

Roshier, B., 'The Selection of Crime News by the Press' in *The*

Manufacture of News, Deviance, Social Problems and the Mass Media, edited by S. Cohen and J. Young, Constable, 1973.

Roth, J., Letter to the *American Sociologist*, vol.4, 1969.

Roth, J., Quoted by A.K. Daniels, 'General Issues' in *The Professions and their Prospects* edited by E. Freidson, Sage, USA, 1971.

Rowe, A., *The School as a Guidance Community*, Pearson, 1971.

Rowntree, J. and Rowntree, M., 'Youth as a Class', *International Socialist Journal*, year 5, no.25, 1968.

Russell, B., *Principles of Social Reconstruction*, Unwin, 1916.

Russell, B., *Power: a New Social Analysis*, W.W. Norton, USA, 1938.

Russell, C.E.M. and Russell, L.M., *'Lads' Clubs*, A. & C. Black, 1932.

Ryder, J. and Silver, H., *Modern English Society 1870-1970*, Methuen, 1970.

Salter-Davies, E., 'The Unemployed Juvenile', *Social Service Review*, no.14, 1933.

Schools Council, *Co-operation Between the Youth Service and the Schools*, Pamphlet no.8, 1971.

Scott, D.M., 'Newson and the Youth Service', *Education*, vol.124, 1964.

Scott, R.A., 'A Proposed Framework for Analysing Deviance as a Property of Social Disorder', in *Theoretical Perspectives on Deviance* edited by R.A. Scott, and J.D. Douglas, Basic Books, USA, 1972.

Seed, P., *The Expansion of Social Work in Britain*, Routledge & Kegan Paul, 1973.

Simon, B., *Education and Labour*, Lawrence & Wishart, 1965.

Simpson, J.A., 'Education and Community Education', *Trends in Education*, no.20, 1970.

Simpson, J.A., *Today and Tomorrow in European Adult Education*, Council of Europe, 1972.

Smith, C., Farrant, M. and Marchant, H., *The Wincroft Youth Project*, Tavistock, 1974.

Smith, D.M., 'The Concept of Youth Culture', *Youth and Society*, vol.7, no.4, 1976.

Smith, G. and James, T., 'The Effects of Pre-School Education', *Oxford Review of Education*, vol.1, no.3, 1975.

Smith, G. and Smith, T., 'The Community School – A Base for Community Development?', in *Community Work One* edited by D. Jones and M. Mays, Routledge & Kegan Paul, 1974.

Smyth, M.L., 'Community Service as an Alternative to Custodial Sentence', unpublished study, Department of Education, Newcastle upon Tyne Polytechnic, 1978.

Springboard, *Springboard in the Context of Youth Unemployment in Sunderland*, Springboard, Toward Road, Sunderland, 1977.

Stanworth, A. and Gidden, A., *Elites and Power in British Society*, Cambridge University Press, 1974.

Stevenson, J., *Social Conditions in Britain Between the Wars*, Penguin, 1977.

Stewart, B., 'A Community Adult Education Service', *Adult Education*, vol.49, 1976.

Storry, J., 'Final Assessment', *Youth Service*, vol.12, 1972.

Sugarman, B., 'Involvement in Youth Culture', *British Journal of Sociology*, vol.18, 1967.

Swados, H., 'Popular Taste and the Agonies of the Young' in *Voices of Dissent*, a collection of articles from *Dissent* Magazine, Grove Press, USA, 1958.

Tawney, R.H., 'Keep the Workers Children in their Place', in *Radical Tradition* (1918). Penguin, 1964.

Tax, M., 'Culture is not Neutral, Whom Does it Serve?', in *Radical Perspectives in the Arts*, edited by L. Baxandall, Penguin, 1972.

Taylor, B., 'Education and the Community', *Youth in Society*, no.14, 1975.

Thompson, E.P., 'Romanticism and Utopianism', *New Left Review*, no.99, 1976.

Thorpe, D., 'Putting Theory into Practice in Ryehill', *Social Work Today*, vol.3, 1972.

Times Educational Supplement, 'Radical Ways to Help Youth', 12 July 1974.

Times Educational Supplement, 'Off the Streets and into the Clubs and Schools', 21 April 1978.

Titmuss, R.M., *Social Policy*, Allen & Unwin, 1974.

Tittle, C.R. and Villemez, W.J., 'Social Class and Criminality', *Social Forces*, vol.56, no.2, 1977.

Toren, N., *Social Work: the Case of a Semi-Profession*, Sage, USA, 1972.

Tremman, J., *Communication and Comprehension*, Longman, 1967.

Trends in Education, 'Community School', April, 1967.

Tweedie, A. *et al.*, *The Report of a Study of the Needs of Young People in Cleator Moor with Particular Reference to their Leisure Time*, Community Development Project, Cleator Moor, 1973.

Tweedie, A., 'There's Nothing to do This Place is Dead', *Youth in Society*, no.5, 1974.

Vaizey, J., *Education for Tomorrow*, Penguin, 1962.

Venables, E., *Teachers and Youth Leaders*, Evans/Methuen, 1971.

Voss, H.L., 'Socio-Economic Status and Reported Delinquent Behaviour', *Social Problems*, no.13, 1966.

Waller, W., *The Sociology of Teaching*, J. Wiley, USA, 1932 and 1965.

Ward, D., 'Personal View', *Social Work Today*, vol.8, no.19, 1977.

Wardle, D., *English Popular Education*, Cambridge University Press, 1970.

Watkins, O., *Professional Training for Youth Work*, Youth Service Information Centre, Leicester, 1972.

Watson, W., *Social and Pastoral Aspects of the Youth Service in Britain*, UNESCO Youth Institute, Munich, 1962.

Watts, J.R. and Whitworth, T.A., *The Professional Youth Leader's View of his Career and Role*, Department of Educational Research, University of Bradford, 1968.

Webb, H., 'The Education Line', *Youth Review*, no.25, 1972.

Webb, J., 'The Sociology of a School', *British Journal of Sociology*, vol.13, 1962.

Westergaard, J. and Resler, H., *Class in a Capitalist Society*, Penguin, 1975.

Widgery, D., *The Left in Britain 1956–1968*, Penguin, 1976.

Wilby, P., 'Education and Equality', *New Statesman*, 17 September 1977.

Williams, R., *The Long Revolution*, Penguin, 1965.

Willmott, P., *Adolescent Boys in East London*, Penguin, 1956.

Wilson-Haffenden, D.J., 'The Boys' Brigade' in *Trends in the Services for Youth* edited by J.H. Leicester and J. Farndale, Pergamon, 1967.

Woolfe, R., 'Simple Questions are Worth Asking', *Youth Review*, no.20, 1971.

Wright, D.O., 'Success in Adult Education', unpublished thesis in Graduate Diploma in Education Studies, University of Leicester, 1975.

Young, G.M., *Victorian England*, Oxford University Press, 1936.

Young, J., 'The Role of the Police as Amplifiers of Deviance, Negotiators of Reality and Translators of Fantasy', in *Images of Deviance* edited by S. Cohen, Penguin, 1970.

Young, M. and Willmott, P., *The Symmetrical Family*, Penguin, 1973.

Younghusband, E., *Social Work in Britain*, Carnegie UK Trust, 1951.

Youth Service Information Centre, *Youth Service Provision for Young Immigrants*, YSIC, 1972.

Youth Service Information Centre, *Youth Work Project Summaries*, YSIC, undated.

Government reports and publications

HMSO (1904), *Report of the Inter-departmental Committee on Physical Deterioration*, vol. One. Cmnd 2175.

HMSO (1919), *Final Report of the Adult Education Committee of the Ministry of Reconstruction*, Cmnd 321.

HMSO (1943), *Youth Service After the War*.

HMSO (1944a), *Teachers and Youth Leaders* (McNair Report).

HMSO (1944b), Education Act (Butler).

HMSO (1944c), *The Purpose and Content of the Youth Service*.

HMSO (1949), *Report of the Committee on the Recruitment, Training and Conditions of Service of Youth Leaders and Community Centre Wardens* (Jackson Report).

HMSO (1951), *Report of the Committee on the Recruitment, Training and Conditions of Service of Youth Leaders and Community Centre Wardens* (Fletcher Report).

HMSO (1960a), *The Youth Service in England and Wales* (Albemarle Report) Cmnd 929.

HMSO (1960b), *15 to 18* (Crowther Report).

HMSO (1962), *The Training of Part-time Youth Leaders and Assistants* (Bessey Report).

HMSO (1963), *Half Our Future* (Newsom Report).

HMSO (1966), *The Second Report on the Training of Part-time Youth Leaders and Assistants*.

HMSO (1967a), *Immigrants and the Youth Service* (Hunt Report).

HMSO (1967b), *Report of the Committee on the Age of Majority* (Latey Committee) Cmnd 3342.

HMSO (1968), *Report of the Committee on Local Authority and Allied Personal Social Services* (Seebohm Report) Cmnd 3703.

HMSO (1968), *Community of Interests* (Scottish Education Department Standing Consultative Council on Youth and Community Service).

HMSO (1969), *Youth and Community Work in the 70s* (Fairbairn-Milson Report).

HMSO (1974), *Unqualified, Untrained and Unemployed.*

HMSO (1976), *Social Trends*, no.7.

HMSO (1976), *Statistics of Education*, vol.1.

Index

Routledge Social Science Series

Routledge & Kegan Paul   London, Henley and Boston

39 Store Street, London WC1E 7DD
Broadway House, Newtown Road,
Henley-on-Thames, Oxon RG9 1EN
9 Park Street, Boston, Mass. 02108

Contents

Authors wishing to submit manuscripts for any series in
this catalogue should send them to the Social Science Editor,
Routledge & Kegan Paul Ltd, 39 Store Street,
London WC1E 7DD

● *Books so marked are available in paperback*
All books are in Metric Demy 8vo format (216 × 138mm approx.)

International Library of Sociology

General Editor John Rex

GENERAL SOCIOLOGY

Barnsley, J. H. The Social Reality of Ethics. *464 pp.*
Brown, Robert. Explanation in Social Science. *208 pp.*
● Rules and Laws in Sociology. *192 pp.*
Bruford, W. H. Chekhov and His Russia. *A Sociological Study. 244 pp.*
Burton, F. and **Carlen, P.** Official Discourse. *On Discourse Analysis, Government Publications, Ideology. About 140 pp.*
Cain, Maureen E. Society and the Policeman's Role. *326 pp.*
●**Fletcher, Colin.** Beneath the Surface. *An Account of Three Styles of Sociological Research. 221 pp.*
Gibson, Quentin. The Logic of Social Enquiry. *240 pp.*
Glucksmann, M. Structuralist Analysis in Contemporary Social Thought. *212 pp.*
Gurvitch, Georges. Sociology of Law. *Foreword by Roscoe Pound. 264 pp.*
Hinkle, R. Founding Theory of American Sociology 1883-1915. *About 350 pp.*
Homans, George C. Sentiments and Activities. *336 pp.*
Johnson, Harry M. Sociology: *a Systematic Introduction. Foreword by Robert K. Merton. 710 pp.*
●**Keat, Russell** and **Urry, John.** Social Theory as Science. *278 pp.*
Mannheim, Karl. Essays on Sociology and Social Psychology. *Edited by Paul Keckskemeti. With Editorial Note by Adolph Lowe. 344 pp.*
Martindale, Don. The Nature and Types of Sociological Theory. *292 pp.*
●**Maus, Heinz.** A Short History of Sociology. *234 pp.*
Myrdal, Gunnar. Value in Social Theory: *A Collection of Essays on Methodology. Edited by Paul Streeten. 332 pp.*
Ogburn, William F. and **Nimkoff, Meyer F.** A Handbook of Sociology. *Preface by Karl Mannheim. 656 pp. 46 figures. 35 tables.*
Parsons, Talcott, and **Smelser, Neil J.** Economy and Society: *A Study in the Integration of Economic and Social Theory. 362 pp.*
Podgórecki, Adam. Practical Social Sciences. *About 200 pp.*
Raffel, S. Matters of Fact. *A Sociological Inquiry. 152 pp.*
●**Rex, John.** (Ed.) Approaches to Sociology. *Contributions by Peter Abell, Sociology and the Demystification of the Modern World. 282 pp.*
●**Rex, John** (Ed.) Approaches to Sociology. *Contributions by Peter Abell, Frank Bechhofer, Basil Bernstein, Ronald Fletcher, David Frisby, Miriam Glucksmann, Peter Lassman, Herminio Martins, John Rex, Roland Robertson, John Westergaard and Jock Young. 302 pp.*
Rigby, A. Alternative Realities. *352 pp.*
Roche, M. Phenomenology, Language and the Social Sciences. *374 pp.*
Sahay, A. Sociological Analysis. *220 pp.*

Strasser, Hermann. The Normative Structure of Sociology. *Conservative and Emancipatory Themes in Social Thought. About 340 pp.*
Strong, P. Ceremonial Order of the Clinic. *About 250 pp.*
Urry, John. Reference Groups and the Theory of Revolution. *244 pp.*
Weinberg, E. Development of Sociology in the Soviet Union. *173 pp.*

FOREIGN CLASSICS OF SOCIOLOGY

● **Gerth, H. H.** and **Mills, C. Wright.** From Max Weber: *Essays in Sociology. 502 pp.*
● **Tönnies, Ferdinand.** Community and Association. *(Gemeinschaft and Gesellschaft.) Translated and Supplemented by Charles P. Loomis. Foreword by Pitirim A. Sorokin. 334 pp.*

SOCIAL STRUCTURE

Andreski, Stanislav. Military Organization and Society. *Foreword by Professor A. R. Radcliffe-Brown. 226 pp. 1 folder.*
Carlton, Eric. Ideology and Social Order. *Foreword by Professor Philip Abrahams. About 320 pp.*
Coontz, Sydney H. Population Theories and the Economic Interpretation. *202 pp.*
Coser, Lewis. The Functions of Social Conflict. *204 pp.*
Dickie-Clark, H. F. Marginal Situation: *A Sociological Study of a Coloured Group. 240 pp. 11 tables.*
Giner, S. and **Archer, M. S.** (Eds.). Contemporary Europe. *Social Structures and Cultural Patterns. 336 pp.*
● **Glaser, Barney** and **Strauss, Anselm L.** Status Passage. *A Formal Theory. 212 pp.*
Glass, D. V. (Ed.) Social Mobility in Britain. *Contributions by J. Berent, T. Bottomore, R. C. Chambers, J. Floud, D. V. Glass, J. R. Hall, H. T. Himmelweit, R. K. Kelsall, F. M. Martin, C. A. Moser, R. Mukherjee, and W. Ziegel. 420 pp.*
Kelsall, R. K. Higher Civil Servants in Britain: *From 1870 to the Present Day. 268 pp. 31 tables.*
● **Lawton, Denis.** Social Class, Language and Education. *192 pp.*
McLeish, John. The Theory of Social Change: *Four Views Considered. 128 pp.*
● **Marsh, David C.** The Changing Social Structure of England and Wales, 1871-1961. *Revised edition. 288 pp.*
Menzies, Ken. Talcott Parsons and the Social Image of Man. *About 208 pp.*
● **Mouzelis, Nicos.** Organization and Bureaucracy. *An Analysis of Modern Theories. 240 pp.*
Ossowski, Stanislaw. Class Structure in the Social Consciousness. *210 pp.*
● **Podgórecki, Adam.** Law and Society. *302 pp.*
Renner, Karl. Institutions of Private Law and Their Social Functions. *Edited, with an Introduction and Notes, by O. Kahn-Freud. Translated by Agnes Schwarzschild. 316 pp.*

Rex, J. and **Tomlinson, S.** Colonial Immigrants in a British City. *A Class Analysis. 368 pp.*
Smooha, S. Israel: Pluralism and Conflict. *472 pp.*
Wesolowski, W. Class, Strata and Power. *Trans. and with Introduction by G. Kolankiewicz. 160 pp.*
Zureik, E. Palestinians in Israel. *A Study in Internal Colonialism. 264 pp.*

SOCIOLOGY AND POLITICS

Acton, T. A. Gypsy Politics and Social Change. *316 pp.*
Burton, F. Politics of Legitimacy. *Struggles in a Belfast Community. 250 pp.*
Etzioni-Halevy, E. Political Manipulation and Administrative Power. *A Comparative Study. About 200 pp.*
● **Hechter, Michael.** Internal Colonialism. *The Celtic Fringe in British National Development, 1536–1966. 380 pp.*
Kornhauser, William. The Politics of Mass Society. *272 pp. 20 tables.*
Korpi, W. The Working Class in Welfare Capitalism. *Work, Unions and Politics in Sweden. 472 pp.*
Kroes, R. Soldiers and Students. *A Study of Right- and Left-wing Students. 174 pp.*
Martin, Roderick. Sociology of Power. *About 272 pp.*
Myrdal, Gunnar. The Political Element in the Development of Economic Theory. *Translated from the German by Paul Streeten. 282 pp.*
Wong, S.-L. Sociology and Socialism in Contemporary China. *160 pp.*
Wootton, Graham. Workers, Unions and the State. *188 pp.*

CRIMINOLOGY

Ancel, Marc. Social Defence: *A Modern Approach to Criminal Problems. Foreword by Leon Radzinowicz. 240 pp.*
Athens, L. Violent Criminal Acts and Actors. *About 150 pp.*
Cain, Maureen E. Society and the Policeman's Role. *326 pp.*
Cloward, Richard A. and **Ohlin, Lloyd E.** Delinquency and Opportunity: *A Theory of Delinquent Gangs. 248 pp.*
Downes, David M. The Delinquent Solution. *A Study in Subcultural Theory. 296 pp.*
Friedlander, Kate. The Psycho-Analytical Approach to Juvenile Delinquency: *Theory, Case Studies, Treatment. 320 pp.*
Gleuck, Sheldon and **Eleanor.** Family Environment and Delinquency. *With the statistical assistance of Rose W. Kneznek. 340 pp.*
Lopez-Rey, Manuel. Crime. *An Analytical Appraisal. 288 pp.*
Mannheim, Hermann. Comparative Criminology: *a Text Book. Two volumes. 442 pp. and 380 pp.*
Morris, Terence. The Criminal Area: *A Study in Social Ecology. Foreword by Hermann Mannheim. 232 pp. 25 tables. 4 maps.*
Podgorecki, A. and **Łos, M.** Multidimensional Sociology. *About 380 pp.*
Rock, Paul. Making People Pay. *338 pp.*

● **Taylor, Ian, Walton, Paul,** and **Young, Jock.** The New Criminology. *For a Social Theory of Deviance. 325 pp.*
● **Taylor, Ian, Walton, Paul** and **Young, Jock.** (Eds) Critical Criminology. *268 pp.*

SOCIAL PSYCHOLOGY

Bagley, Christopher. The Social Psychology of the Epileptic Child. *320 pp.*
Brittan, Arthur. Meanings and Situations. *224 pp.*
Carroll, J. Break-Out from the Crystal Palace. *200 pp.*
● **Fleming, C. M.** Adolescence: Its Social Psychology. *With an Introduction to recent findings from the fields of Anthropology, Physiology, Medicine, Psychometrics and Sociometry. 288 pp.*
● The Social Psychology of Education: *An Introduction and Guide to Its Study. 136 pp.*
Linton, Ralph. The Cultural Background of Personality. *132 pp.*
● **Mayo, Elton.** The Social Problems of an Industrial Civilization. *With an Appendix on the Political Problem. 180 pp.*
Ottaway, A. K. C. Learning Through Group Experience. *176 pp.*
Plummer, Ken. Sexual Stigma. *An Interactionist Account. 254 pp.*
● **Rose, Arnold M.** (Ed.) Human Behaviour and Social Processes: *an Interactionist Approach. Contributions by Arnold M. Rose, Ralph H. Turner, Anselm Strauss, Everett C. Hughes, E. Franklin Frazier, Howard S. Becker et al. 696 pp.*
Smelser, Neil J. Theory of Collective Behaviour. *448 pp.*
Stephenson, Geoffrey M. The Development of Conscience. *128 pp.*
Young, Kimball. Handbook of Social Psychology. *658 pp. 16 figures. 10 tables.*

SOCIOLOGY OF THE FAMILY

Bell, Colin R. Middle Class Families: *Social and Geographical Mobility. 224 pp.*
Burton, Lindy. Vulnerable Children. *272 pp.*
Gavron, Hannah. The Captive Wife: *Conflicts of Household Mothers. 190 pp.*
George, Victor and **Wilding, Paul.** Motherless Families. *248 pp.*
Klein, Josephine. Samples from English Cultures.
  1. Three Preliminary Studies and Aspects of Adult Life in England. *447 pp.*
  2. Child-Rearing Practices and Index. *247 pp.*
Klein, Viola. The Feminine Character. *History of an Ideology. 244 pp.*
McWhinnie, Alexina M. Adopted Children. *How They Grow Up. 304 pp.*
● **Morgan, D. H. J.** Social Theory and the Family. *About 320 pp.*
● **Myrdal, Alva** and **Klein, Viola.** Women's Two Roles: *Home and Work. 238 pp. 27 tables.*

Parsons, Talcott and **Bales, Robert F.** Family: Socialization and Inter-action Process. *In collaboration with James Olds, Morris Zelditch and Philip E. Slater. 456 pp. 50 figures and tables.*

SOCIAL SERVICES

Bastide, Roger. The Sociology of Mental Disorder. *Translated from the French by Jean McNeil. 260 pp.*

Carlebach, Julius. Caring For Children in Trouble. *266 pp.*

George, Victor. Foster Care. *Theory and Practice. 234 pp.*
Social Security: *Beveridge and After. 258 pp.*

George, V. and **Wilding, P.** Motherless Families. *248 pp.*

● **Goetschius, George W.** Working with Community Groups. *256 pp.*

Goetschius, George W. and **Tash, Joan.** Working with Unattached Youth. *416 pp.*

Heywood, Jean S. Children in Care. *The Development of the Service for the Deprived Child. Third revised edition. 284 pp.*

King, Roy D., Ranes, Norma V. and **Tizard, Jack.** Patterns of Residential Care. *356 pp.*

Leigh, John. Young People and Leisure. *256 pp.*

● **Mays, John.** (Ed.) Penelope Hall's Social Services of England and Wales. *About 324 pp.*

Morris, Mary. Voluntary Work and the Welfare State. *300 pp.*

Nokes, P. L. The Professional Task in Welfare Practice. *152 pp.*

Timms, Noel. Psychiatric Social Work in Great Britain (1939-1962). *280 pp.*

● Social Casework: *Principles and Practice. 256 pp.*

SOCIOLOGY OF EDUCATION

Banks, Olive. Parity and Prestige in English Secondary Education: a Study in Educational Sociology. *272 pp.*

● **Blyth, W. A. L.** English Primary Education. *A Sociological Description.* 2. Background. *168 pp.*

Collier, K. G. The Social Purposes of Education: *Personal and Social Values in Education. 268 pp.*

Evans, K. M. Sociometry and Education. *158 pp.*

● **Ford, Julienne.** Social Class and the Comprehensive School. *192 pp.*

Foster, P. J. Education and Social Change in Ghana. *336 pp. 3 maps.*

Fraser, W. R. Education and Society in Modern France. *150 pp.*

Grace, Gerald R. Role Conflict and the Teacher. *150 pp.*

Hans, Nicholas. New Trends in Education in the Eighteenth Century. *278 pp. 19 tables.*

● Comparative Education: *A Study of Educational Factors and Traditions. 360 pp.*

● **Hargreaves, David.** Interpersonal Relations and Education. *432 pp.*

● Social Relations in a Secondary School. *240 pp.*

School Organization and Pupil Involvement. *A Study of Secondary Schools.*

● **Mannheim, Karl** and **Stewart, W.A.C.** An Introduction to the Sociology of Education. *206 pp.*
● **Musgrove, F.** Youth and the Social Order. *176 pp.*
● **Ottaway, A. K. C.** Education and Society: An Introduction to the Sociology of Education. *With an Introduction by W. O. Lester Smith. 212 pp.*
  Peers, Robert. Adult Education: *A Comparative Study. Revised edition. 398 pp.*
  Stratta, Erica. The Education of Borstal Boys. *A Study of their Educational Experiences prior to, and during, Borstal Training. 256 pp.*
● **Taylor, P. H., Reid, W. A.** and **Holley, B. J.** The English Sixth Form. *A Case Study in Curriculum Research. 198 pp.*

SOCIOLOGY OF CULTURE

Eppel, E. M. and **M.** Adolescents and Morality: *A Study of some Moral Values and Dilemmas of Working Adolescents in the Context of a changing Climate of Opinion. Foreword by W. J. H. Sprott. 268 pp. 39 tables.*
● **Fromm, Erich.** The Fear of Freedom. *286 pp.*
●   The Sane Society. *400 pp.*
  Johnson, L. The Cultural Critics. *From Matthew Arnold to Raymond Williams. 233 pp.*
  Mannheim, Karl. Essays on the Sociology of Culture. *Edited by Ernst Mannheim in co-operation with Paul Kecskemeti. Editorial Note by Adolph Lowe. 280 pp.*
  Zijderfeld, A. C. On Clichés. *The Supersedure of Meaning by Function in Modernity. About 132 pp.*

SOCIOLOGY OF RELIGION

Argyle, Michael and **Beit-Hallahmi, Benjamin.** The Social Psychology of Religion. *About 256 pp.*
Glasner, Peter E. The Sociology of Secularisation. *A Critique of a Concept. About 180 pp.*
Hall, J. R. The Ways Out. *Utopian Communal Groups in an Age of Babylon. 280 pp.*
Ranson, S., Hinings, B. and **Bryman, A.** Clergy, Ministers and Priests. *216 pp.*
Stark, Werner. The Sociology of Religion. *A Study of Christendom.*
  Volume II. *Sectarian Religion. 368 pp.*
  Volume III. *The Universal Church. 464 pp.*
  Volume IV. *Types of Religious Man. 352 pp.*
  Volume V. *Types of Religious Culture. 464 pp.*
Turner, B. S. Weber and Islam. *216 pp.*
Watt, W. Montgomery. Islam and the Integration of Society. *320 pp.*

SOCIOLOGY OF ART AND LITERATURE

Jarvie, Ian C. Towards a Sociology of the Cinema. *A Comparative Essay on the Structure and Functioning of a Major Entertainment Industry. 405 pp.*

Rust, Frances S. Dance in Society. *An Analysis of the Relationships between the Social Dance and Society in England from the Middle Ages to the Present Day. 256 pp. 8 pp. of plates.*

Schücking, L. L. The Sociology of Literary Taste. *112 pp.*

Wolff, Janet. Hermeneutic Philosophy and the Sociology of Art. *150 pp.*

SOCIOLOGY OF KNOWLEDGE

Diesing, P. Patterns of Discovery in the Social Sciences. *262 pp.*

● **Douglas, J. D.** (Ed.) Understanding Everyday Life. *370 pp.*

Glasner, B. Essential Interactionism. *About 220 pp.*

● **Hamilton, P.** Knowledge and Social Structure. *174 pp.*

Jarvie, I. C. Concepts and Society. *232 pp.*

Mannheim, Karl. Essays on the Sociology of Knowledge. *Edited by Paul Kecskemeti. Editorial Note by Adolph Lowe. 353 pp.*

Remmling, Gunter W. The Sociology of Karl Mannheim. *With a Bibliographical Guide to the Sociology of Knowledge, Ideological Analysis, and Social Planning. 255 pp.*

Remmling, Gunter W. (Ed.) Towards the Sociology of Knowledge. *Origin and Development of a Sociological Thought Style. 463 pp.*

URBAN SOCIOLOGY

Aldridge, M. The British New Towns. *A Programme Without a Policy. About 250 pp.*

Ashworth, William. The Genesis of Modern British Town Planning: *A Study in Economic and Social History of the Nineteenth and Twentieth Centuries. 288 pp.*

Brittan, A. The Privatised World. *196 pp.*

Cullingworth, J. B. Housing Needs and Planning Policy: *A Restatement of the Problems of Housing Need and 'Overspill' in England and Wales. 232 pp. 44 tables. 8 maps.*

Dickinson, Robert E. City and Region: *A Geographical Interpretation. 608 pp. 125 figures.*

The West European City: *A Geographical Interpretation. 600 pp. 129 maps. 29 plates.*

Humphreys, Alexander J. New Dubliners: *Urbanization and the Irish Family. Foreword by George C. Homans. 304 pp.*

Jackson, Brian. Working Class Community: *Some General Notions raised by a Series of Studies in Northern England. 192 pp.*

● **Mann, P. H.** An Approach to Urban Sociology. *240 pp.*

Mellor, J. R. Urban Sociology in an Urbanized Society. *326 pp.*

Morris, R. N. and **Mogey, J.** The Sociology of Housing. *Studies at Berinsfield. 232 pp. 4 pp. plates.*

Rosser, C. and **Harris, C.** The Family and Social Change. *A Study of Family and Kinship in a South Wales Town. 352 pp. 8 maps.*

● **Stacey, Margaret, Batsone, Eric, Bell, Colin** and **Thurcott, Anne.** Power, Persistence and Change. *A Second Study of Banbury. 196 pp.*

RURAL SOCIOLOGY

Mayer, Adrian C. Peasants in the Pacific. *A Study of Fiji Indian Rural Society. 248 pp. 20 plates.*

Williams, W. M. The Sociology of an English Village: *Gosforth. 272 pp. 12 figures. 13 tables.*

SOCIOLOGY OF INDUSTRY AND DISTRIBUTION

Dunkerley, David. The Foreman. *Aspects of Task and Structure. 192 pp.*

Eldridge, J. E. T. Industrial Disputes. *Essays in the Sociology of Industrial Relations. 288 pp.*

Hollowell, Peter G. The Lorry Driver. *272 pp.*

● **Oxaal, I., Barnett, T.** and **Booth, D.** (Eds) Beyond the Sociology of Development. *Economy and Society in Latin America and Africa. 295 pp.*

Smelser, Neil J. Social Change in the Industrial Revolution: *An Application of Theory to the Lancashire Cotton Industry, 1770–1840. 468 pp. 12 figures. 14 tables.*

Watson, T. J. The Personnel Managers. *A Study in the Sociology of Work and Employment. 262 pp.*

ANTHROPOLOGY

Brandel-Syrier, Mia. Reeftown Elite. *A Study of Social Mobility in a Modern African Community on the Reef. 376 pp.*

Dickie-Clark, H. F. The Marginal Situation. *A Sociological Study of a Coloured Group. 236 pp.*

Dube, S. C. Indian Village. *Foreword by Morris Edward Opler. 276 pp. 4 plates.*

India's Changing Villages: *Human Factors in Community Development. 260 pp. 8 plates. 1 map.*

Firth, Raymond. Malay Fishermen. *Their Peasant Economy. 420 pp. 17 pp. plates.*

Gulliver, P. H. Social Control in an African Society: a Study of the Arusha, Agricultural Masai of Northern Tanganyika. *320 pp. 8 plates. 10 figures.*

Family Herds. *288 pp.*

Jarvie, Ian C. The Revolution in Anthropology. *268 pp.*

Little, Kenneth L. Mende of Sierra Leone. *308 pp. and folder.*

Negroes in Britain. *With a New Introduction and Contemporary Study by Leonard Bloom. 320 pp.*

Madan, G. R. Western Sociologists on Indian Society. *Marx, Spencer, Weber, Durkheim, Pareto. 384 pp.*

Mayer, A. C. Peasants in the Pacific. *A Study of Fiji Indian Rural Society. 248 pp.*

Meer, Fatima. Race and Suicide in South Africa. *325 pp.*

Smith, Raymond T. The Negro Family in British Guiana: *Family Structure and Social Status in the Villages. With a Foreword by Meyer Fortes. 314 pp. 8 plates. 1 figure. 4 maps.*

SOCIOLOGY AND PHILOSOPHY

Barnsley, John H. The Social Reality of Ethics. *A Comparative Analysis of Moral Codes. 448 pp.*

Diesing, Paul. Patterns of Discovery in the Social Sciences. *362 pp.*

● **Douglas, Jack D.** (Ed.) Understanding Everyday Life. *Toward the Reconstruction of Sociological Knowledge. Contributions by Alan F. Blum, Aaron W. Cicourel, Norman K. Denzin, Jack D. Douglas, John Heeren, Peter McHugh, Peter K. Manning, Melvin Power, Matthew Speier, Roy Turner, D. Lawrence Wieder, Thomas P. Wilson and Don H. Zimmerman. 370 pp.*

Gorman, Robert A. The Dual Vision. *Alfred Schutz and the Myth of Phenomenological Social Science. About 300 pp.*

Jarvie, Ian C. Concepts and Society. *216 pp.*

Kilminster, R. Praxis and Method. *A Sociological Dialogue with Lukács, Gramsci and the early Frankfurt School. About 304 pp.*

● **Pelz, Werner.** The Scope of Understanding in Sociology. *Towards a More Radical Reorientation in the Social Humanistic Sciences. 283 pp.*

Roche, Maurice. Phenomenology, Language and the Social Sciences. *371 pp.*

Sahay, Arun. Sociological Analysis. *212 pp.*

Slater, P. Origin and Significance of the Frankfurt School. *A Marxist Perspective. About 192 pp.*

Spurling, L. Phenomenology and the Social World. *The Philosophy of Merleau-Ponty and its Relation to the Social Sciences. 222 pp.*

Wilson, H. T. The American Ideology. *Science, Technology and Organization as Modes of Rationality. 368 pp.*

International Library of Anthropology

General Editor Adam Kuper

Ahmed, A. S. Millenium and Charisma Among Pathans. *A Critical Essay in Social Anthropology. 192 pp.*
Pukhtun Economy and Society. *About 360 pp.*

Brown, Paula. The Chimbu. *A Study of Change in the New Guinea Highlands. 151 pp.*
Foner, N. Jamaica Farewell. *200 pp.*
Gudeman, Stephen. Relationships, Residence and the Individual. *A Rural Panamanian Community. 288 pp. 11 plates, 5 figures, 2 maps, 10 tables.*
The Demise of a Rural Economy. *From Subsistence to Capitalism in a Latin American Village. 160 pp.*
Hamnett, Ian. Chieftainship and Legitimacy. *An Anthropological Study of Executive Law in Lesotho. 163 pp.*
Hanson, F. Allan. Meaning in Culture. *127 pp.*
Humphreys, S. C. Anthropology and the Greeks. *288 pp.*
Karp, I. Fields of Change Among the Iteso of Kenya. *140 pp.*
Lloyd, P. C. Power and Independence. *Urban Africans' Perception of Social Inequality. 264 pp.*
Parry, J. P. Caste and Kinship in Kangra. *352 pp. Illustrated.*
Pettigrew, Joyce. Robber Noblemen. *A Study of the Political System of the Sikh Jats. 284 pp.*
Street, Brian V. The Savage in Literature. *Representations of 'Primitive' Society in English Fiction, 1858–1920. 207 pp.*
Van Den Berghe, Pierre L. Power and Privilege at an African University. *278 pp.*

International Library of Social Policy

General Editor Kathleen Jones

Bayley, M. Mental Handicap and Community Care. *426 pp.*
Bottoms, A. E. and **McClean, J. D.** Defendants in the Criminal Process. *284 pp.*
Butler, J. R. Family Doctors and Public Policy. *208 pp.*
Davies, Martin. Prisoners of Society. *Attitudes and Aftercare. 204 pp.*
Gittus, Elizabeth. Flats, Families and the Under-Fives. *285 pp.*
Holman, Robert. Trading in Children. *A Study of Private Fostering. 355 pp.*
Jeffs, A. Young People and the Youth Service. *About 180 pp.*
Jones, Howard, and **Cornes, Paul.** Open Prisons. *288 pp.*
Jones, Kathleen. History of the Mental Health Service. *428 pp.*
Jones, Kathleen, with **Brown, John, Cunningham, W. J., Roberts, Julian** and **Williams, Peter.** Opening the Door. *A Study of New Policies for the Mentally Handicapped. 278 pp.*
Karn, Valerie. Retiring to the Seaside. *About 280 pp. 2 maps. Numerous tables.*
King, R. D. and **Elliot, K. W.** Albany: Birth of a Prison—End of an Era. *394 pp.*

Thomas, J. E. The English Prison Officer since 1850: *A Study in Conflict.* *258 pp.*

Walton, R. G. Women in Social Work. *303 pp.*

● **Woodward, J.** To Do the Sick No Harm. *A Study of the British Voluntary Hospital System to 1875. 234 pp.*

International Library of Welfare and Philosophy

General Editors   Noel Timms and David Watson

● **McDermott, F. E.** (Ed.) Self-Determination in Social Work. *A Collection of Essays on Self-determination and Related Concepts by Philosophers and Social Work Theorists. Contributors: F. B. Biestek, S. Bernstein, A. Keith-Lucas, D. Sayer, H. H. Perelman, C. Whittington, R. F. Stalley, F. E. McDermott, I. Berlin, H. J. McCloskey, H. L. A. Hart, J. Wilson, A. I. Melden, S. I. Benn. 254 pp.*

● **Plant, Raymond.** Community and Ideology. *104 pp.*

Ragg, Nicholas M. People Not Cases. *A Philosophical Approach to Social Work. About 250 pp.*

● **Timms, Noel** and **Watson, David.** (Eds) Talking About Welfare. *Readings in Philosophy and Social Policy. Contributors: T. H. Marshall, R. B. Brandt, G. H. von Wright, K. Nielsen, M. Cranston, R. M. Titmuss, R. S. Downie, E. Telfer, D. Donnison, J. Benson, P. Leonard, A. Keith-Lucas, D. Walsh, I. T. Ramsey. 320 pp.*

●   (Eds). Philosophy in Social Work. *250 pp.*

● **Weale, A.** Equality and Social Policy. *164 pp.*

Primary Socialization, Language and Education

General Editor   Basil Bernstein

Adlam, Diana S., *with the assistance of Geoffrey Turner and Lesley Lineker.* Code in Context. *About 272 pp.*

Bernstein, Basil. Class, Codes and Control. *3 volumes.*

●   1. *Theoretical Studies Towards a Sociology of Language. 254 pp.*

   2. *Applied Studies Towards a Sociology of Language. 377 pp.*

●   3. *Towards a Theory of Educational Transmission. 167 pp.*

Brandis, W. and **Bernstein, B.** Selection and Control. *176 pp.*

Brandis, Walter and **Henderson, Dorothy.** Social Class, Language and Communication. *288 pp.*

Cook-Gumperz, Jenny. Social Control and Socialization. *A Study of Class Differences in the Language of Maternal Control. 290 pp.*

● **Gahagan, D. M** and **G. A.** Talk Reform. *Exploration in Language for Infant School Children. 160 pp.*

Hawkins, P. R. Social Class, the Nominal Group and Verbal Strategies. *About 220 pp.*

Robinson, W. P. and **Rackstraw, Susan D. A.** A Question of Answers. *2 volumes. 192 pp. and 180 pp.*

Turner, Geoffrey J. and **Mohan, Bernard A.** A Linguistic Description and Computer Programme for Children's Speech. *208 pp.*

Reports of the Institute of Community Studies

Baker, J. The Neighbourhood Advice Centre. A Community Project in Camden. *320 pp.*

● **Cartwright, Ann.** Patients and their Doctors. *A Study of General Practice. 304 pp.*

Dench, Geoff. Maltese in London. *A Case-study in the Erosion of Ethnic Consciousness. 302 pp.*

Jackson, Brian and **Marsden, Dennis.** Education and the Working Class: *Some General Themes raised by a Study of 88 Working-class Children in a Northern Industrial City. 268 pp. 2 folders.*

Marris, Peter. The Experience of Higher Education. *232 pp. 27 tables.*

● Loss and Change. *192 pp.*

Marris, Peter and **Rein, Martin.** Dilemmas of Social Reform. *Poverty and Community Action in the United States. 256 pp.*

Marris, Peter and **Somerset, Anthony.** African Businessmen. *A Study of Entrepreneurship and Development in Keyna. 256 pp.*

Mills, Richard. Young Outsiders: *a Study in Alternative Communities. 216 pp.*

Runciman, W. G. Relative Deprivation and Social Justice. *A Study of Attitudes to Social Inequality in Twentieth-Century England. 352 pp.*

Willmott, Peter. Adolescent Boys in East London. *230 pp.*

Willmott, Peter and **Young, Michael.** Family and Class in a London Suburb. *202 pp. 47 tables.*

Young, Michael and **McGeeney, Patrick.** Learning Begins at Home. *A Study of a Junior School and its Parents. 128 pp.*

Young, Michael and **Willmott, Peter.** Family and Kinship in East London. *Foreword by Richard M. Titmuss. 252 pp. 39 tables.*

The Symmetrical Family. *410 pp.*

Reports of the Institute for Social Studies in Medical Care

Cartwright, Ann, Hockey, Lisbeth and **Anderson, John J.** Life Before Death. *310 pp.*

Dunnell, Karen and **Cartwright, Ann.** Medicine Takers, Prescribers and Hoarders. *190 pp.*

Farrell, C. My Mother Said. . . . *A Study of the Way Young People Learned About Sex and Birth Control. 200 pp.*

Medicine, Illness and Society

General Editor W. M. Williams

Hall, David J. Social Relations & Innovation. *Changing the State of Play in Hospitals. 232 pp.*

Hall, David J., and **Stacey, M.** (Eds) Beyond Separation. *234 pp.*

Robinson, David. The Process of Becoming Ill. *142 pp.*

Stacey, Margaret *et al.* Hospitals, Children and Their Families. *The Report of a Pilot Study. 202 pp.*

Stimson G. V. and **Webb, B.** Going to See the Doctor. *The Consultation Process in General Practice. 155 pp.*

Monographs in Social Theory

General Editor Arthur Brittan

● **Barnes, B.** Scientific Knowledge and Sociological Theory. *192 pp.*

Bauman, Zygmunt. Culture as Praxis. *204 pp.*

● **Dixon, Keith.** Sociological Theory. *Pretence and Possibility. 142 pp.*

Meltzer, B. N., Petras, J. W. and **Reynolds, L. T.** Symbolic Interactionism. *Genesis, Varieties and Criticisms. 144 pp.*

● **Smith, Anthony D.** The Concept of Social Change. *A Critique of the Functionalist Theory of Social Change. 208 pp.*

Routledge Social Science Journals

The British Journal of Sociology. *Editor – Angus Stewart; Associate Editor – Leslie Sklair. Vol. 1, No. 1 – March 1950 and Quarterly. Roy. 8vo. All back issues available. An international journal publishing original papers in the field of sociology and related areas.*

Community Work. *Edited by David Jones and Marjorie Mayo. 1973. Published annually.*

Economy and Society. *Vol. 1, No. 1. February 1972 and Quarterly. Metric Roy. 8vo. A journal for all social scientists covering sociology, philosophy, anthropology, economics and history. All back numbers available.*

Ethnic and Racial Studies. *Editor – John Stone. Vol. 1 – 1978. Published quarterly.*

Religion. Journal of Religion and Religions. *Chairman of Editorial Board, Ninian Smart. Vol. 1, No. 1, Spring 1971. A journal with an interdisciplinary approach to the study of the phenomena of religion. All back numbers available.*

Sociology of Health and Illness. *A Journal of Medical Sociology. Editor – Alan Davies; Associate Editor – Ray Jobling. Vol. 1, Spring 1979. Published 3 times per annum.*

Year Book of Social Policy in Britain, The. *Edited by Kathleen Jones. 1971. Published annually.*

Social and Psychological Aspects of Medical Practice

Editor Trevor Silverstone

Lader, Malcolm. Psychophysiology of Mental Illness. *280 pp.*

● **Silverstone, Trevor** and **Turner, Paul.** Drug Treatment in Psychiatry. *Revised edition. 256 pp.*

Whiteley, J. S. and **Gordon, J.** Group Approaches in Psychiatry. *256 pp.*

Printed in Great Britain by
Lowe & Brydone Printers Limited, Thetford, Norfolk